Furthering the Quest
for Peace

Milton Pierce

PRIME MINISTER FOR PEACE

PRIME MINISTER FOR PEACE

My Struggle for Serbian Democracy

Milan Panic

with Kevin C. Murphy

ROWMAN & LITTLEFIELD
Lanham • Boulder • New York • London

Published by Rowman & Littlefield
A wholly owned subsidiary of
The Rowman & Littlefield Publishing Group, Inc.
4501 Forbes Boulevard, Suite 200, Lanham, Maryland 20706
www.rowman.com

Unit A, Whitacre Mews, 26-34 Stannary Street, London SE11 4AB,
United Kingdom

British Library Cataloguing in Publication Information Available

Library of Congress Cataloging-in-Publication Data
Panic, Milan, 1929–
Prime minister for peace : my struggle for Serbian democracy / Milan Panic, as told to Kevin C.
Murphy ; foreword by Bill Press.
pages cm
Summary: "In this remarkable memoir, Milan Panic tells the formerly unknown story of his at-
tempts to oust Slobodan Milosevic and his battles with the U.S. State Department in an effort to
bring peace to the Balkans during the Yugoslav Wars. A young cycling champion who fought the
Nazi occupation in Yugoslavia with Tito's partisans, Panic defected after World War II from his
now-communist country to start a new life in the United States. But his greatest challenge still lay
ahead when he was invited to serve as prime minister of Yugoslavia. But in Belgrade, ancient
enmities and suspicions festered, and the threat of tragedy and bloodshed loomed large as ethnic
conflict raged. And even as Panic implored the West for support, he would have to outwit the
machinations of a wily Serbian dictator, Slobodan Milosevic. Including behind-the-scenes details
of his rivalry with Milosevic, this book is a compelling chronicle of the road to peace in the
Balkans"—Provided by publisher.
Includes index.
ISBN 978-1-4422-4362-0 (cloth : alkaline paper) — ISBN 978-1-4422-4363-7 (electronic)
1. Panic, Milan, 1929- 2. Prime ministers—Yugoslavia—Biography. 3. Yugoslavia—Politics and
government—1992-2003. 4. Milosevic, Slobodan, 1941-2006—Adversaries. 5. Serbia—Politics and
government—1992-2006. 6. Democracy—Serbia. 7. Peace-building—Balkan Peninsula. 8. Yugoslav Americans—Biography. 9. Immigrants—United States—Biography. I. Murphy, Kevin C.,
1974- II. Title.
DR1321.P36A3 2015
949.7103'1092—dc23
[B]
2014038246

Printed in the United States of America

DRAMATIS PERSONAE

Albright, Madeleine – U.S. ambassador to the United Nations and later secretary of state in the Clinton administration. She was the first woman to serve in that position.

Avramovic, Dragoslav – Former World Bank economist who, at Milosevic's behest, became head of Yugoslavia's Central Bank and helped to stabilize the economy. Affectionately known to many Serbians as "Grandpa Avram," he later became the public face of the opposition coalition Zajedno (Together).

Baker, James – Secretary of state under, and close aide to, George H. W. Bush; ultimately replaced by Lawrence Eagleburger.

Bayh, Birch – Lawyer, former U.S. senator from Arkansas; friend and advisor to Panic before, during, and after his tenure as Yugoslavia's prime minister.

Bildt, Carl – Former Swedish prime minister; eventually replaced David Owen as chief peace negotiator in the Balkans for the European Union.

Calef, David – Former ICN manager who served as Milan Panic's press officer during his time as prime minister.

Carrington, Lord (Peter) – Former British foreign secretary; served as the European Union's peace envoy to the former Yugoslavia.

Christopher, Warren – Secretary of state under Bill Clinton.

Clark, Wesley – American general and head of NATO forces as Supreme Allied Commander Europe; presided over NATO military operations during the Kosovo War.

Cosic, Dobrica – First president of the Federal Republic of Yugoslavia; novelist and advocate of Serbian nationalism; key political player during Panic's time in the country.

Djindjic, Zoran – Serbian politician and cofounder of the Democratic Party; later served as Yugoslavia's prime minister.

Djukanovic, Milo – Prime minister of Montenegro and a key political opponent of Slobodan Milosevic; later served as both prime minister and president of an independent Montenegro.

Draskovic, Vuk – Opposition leader who, along with his wife, was beaten and imprisoned by the Milosevic regime; later served in the Milosevic cabinet during the Kosovo conflict.

Eagleburger, Lawrence – Former ambassador to Yugoslavia and veteran diplomat; eventually appointed as George H. W. Bush's secretary of state.

Fuerth, Leon – Foreign policy advisor to Vice President Al Gore.

Gelbard, Robert – Senior State Department official and envoy to the Balkans during the Clinton administration.

Holbrooke, Richard – Veteran diplomat sent as a personal envoy of President Clinton to the Balkans, with full negotiating power to defuse the crises in the region; later served as UN ambassador from 1999 to 2001.

Izetbegovic, Alija – Lawyer, author, and Bosnian Muslim politician who served as the first president of Bosnia and Herzegovina beginning in 1990.

Jerney, Adam – One of Panic's top lieutenants at ICN.

Jovanovic, Vladislav – Milosevic ally who served as foreign minister during Milan Panic's term as prime minister.

Karadzic, Radovan – Head of the Bosnian Serbs, tacitly supported by Slobodan Milosevic.

Kertes, Mihaly – First deputy interior minister and head of the federal secret police; a close ally of Milosevic and his wife, he had supervised covert ethnic cleansing operations in Bosnia and Serbia.

Kesic, Obrac – Young Serbian American aide to Panic; ran Panic's government affairs office in Washington, D.C., beginning in 1998. There, he worked to train and encourage support for democratic opposition activists in Serbia.

Khan, Rafi – California broker who, soon after Panic's time as prime minister, attempted a hostile takeover of ICN Pharmaceuticals that ultimately failed.

Kitic, Melena – Star of the Belgrade Opera; became Milan Panic's third wife.

Koljevic, Nikola – Bosnian Serb vice president during the Bosnian War.

Kontic, Radoje – Milan Panic's successor as prime minister of Yugoslavia, served from 1993 to 1998.

Kostunica, Vojislav – Leader of the Democratic Party of Serbia; eventually became the opposition coalition candidate for Serbia's president and successfully defeated Slobodan Milosevic in 2000.

Markovic, Mirijana – Wife and close political ally of Slobodan Milosevic.

Milosevic, Slobodan – President of Serbia, who rose to and held dictatorial power in Yugoslavia by inflaming ethnic tensions and Serbian nationalism.

Mitevic, Dusan – Director of Radio Television of Serbia, the official Serbian state media, and key Milosevic aide; Mitevic was privy to, and later disavowed, Milosevic's promise to Panic that the dictator would step down.

Mladic, Ratko – Bosnian Serb military commander responsible for the massacre at Srebrenica.

Montgomery, William – Key assistant to Lawrence Eagleburger; later became President Clinton's ambassador to Yugoslavia.

Narandzic, Jelica – Panic's first wife, who fled Yugoslavia and emigrated with him to California; she died in 1976.

O'Hagan, Marcia – Longtime personal assistant to Milan Panic, both at ICN and in Belgrade.

Olic, Ted – Old friend of Panic; served as ICN vice president and later became an important aide during Panic's prime ministry.

Owen, Lord (David) – Former British foreign secretary; represented the European Union in peace negotiations in the Balkans after Lord Carrington.

Panic, Milan – Serbian-born American businessman, founder and chairman of ICN Pharmaceuticals, and the protagonist of this tale, Panic—as prime minister of Yugoslavia, presidential candidate, and democratic activist in exile—championed peace and political and economic reforms in the Balkans and challenged Slobodan Milosevic's hold on power.

Panic, Sally – Milan Panic's second wife.

Panic, Zivota – Chief of staff and key military commander in Belgrade, as well as regular tennis partner of Milan Panic (no relation).

Press, Bill – Former chair of the California Democratic Party, author and longtime radio and television talk-show host, and friend to Milan Panic; helped Panic with his television advertising during the latter's presidential candidacy.

Rakic, Ljubisa – Noted scientist and old friend of Milan Panic who (despite Milosevic's objections) served as deputy prime minister and a key diplomatic aide to Panic during his tenure in Yugoslavia.

Rugova, Ibrahim – Poet and leader of the Albanian opposition to Serb rule in Kosovo.

Scanlan, John D. – Former ambassador to Yugoslavia and a veteran State Department hand; served as a key aide to Milan Panic during his time in Belgrade.

Schoen, Doug – American pollster who, while examining the prospects for Panic's presidential candidacy and thereafter, identified tepid support for Milosevic in Serbia.

Seselj, Vojislav – Head of the ultranationalist Radical Party in Serbia; key supporter of the Milosevic regime.

Smith, Roberts – UCLA biochemistry professor and one of Panic's earliest backers; became a trusted top executive at ICN.

Stamenkovic, Momo – Cousin of Milan Panic with whom he and Jelica lived in Huntington Beach just after the move to California.

Tito, Josef – Leader of the Yugoslavian partisans during World War II, he ruled as marshal (supreme military commander) and president over Communist Yugoslavia from the end of the war to 1980.

Tudjman, Franjo – President of Croatia.

Ulepic, Zdenko – Officer in the Yugoslavia military during and after WWII; Panic served as his personal aide.

Vance, Cyrus – Former U.S. secretary of state under Jimmy Carter; appointed as UN peace negotiator to Croatia.

Varady, Tibory – Law professor who served as minister of justice under Milan Panic.

Vucelic, Milorad – Director general of Radio Television Belgrade after Dusan Mitevic.

Vukcevic, Dmitri – Serbian American serving as security for Panic during his time as prime minister.

Zimmermann, Warren – Ambassador to Yugoslavia under Presidents Bush and Clinton; resigned in 1994.

FOREWORD

Bill Press

To say the least, Milan Panic is one of the most interesting people I've ever met. He's also one of the most energetic, optimistic, determined, generous, stubborn, relentless, successful, daring, demanding, and sometimes reckless people I've ever met. This can make for a volatile mix, indeed! And yet it is this same unique concoction of characteristics that has propelled him to success in the business world, and that thrust him, at a very delicate time in Yugoslavia's history, onto the world stage.

As this book relates, Milan is, first of all, a true American success story. Born in Belgrade, a member of his country's national cycling team and a champion of Yugoslavia, he defected from his homeland while traveling to a 1955 international competition in the Netherlands. A year later, he arrived in New York with his wife and young family, two suitcases, and $20 in his pocket. From the East Coast, he made his way to Los Angeles, where he worked in the chemistry lab at USC for four years. In 1959, with $200 cash, he founded ICN Pharmaceuticals, which he built into a multibillion-dollar business until he resigned as chairman in 2002. Today, he's still going strong as CEO of MP Biomedicals, with operations in the United States, Europe, South America, China, and throughout the Pacific.

Despite all the demands of his worldwide enterprise, Milan's also the kind of devoted father who would take ten days off from everything else just to accompany his son on a whirlwind visit of the museums, monuments, and historical sites of Washington, D.C., because that's what his son wanted for his twelfth birthday present. The apple does not fall far from the tree!

As a businessman, Milan was never content with making it big in the American market. Ever looking for new business opportunities, he saw his first opening to expand outside the United States with the collapse of Communism in Eastern Europe. He began in his old homeland of Serbia, buying the state-owned pharmaceutical company Galenika; converting it to a subsidiary of his public company listed on the New York Stock Exchange; and, for the first time anywhere in Eastern Europe, offering his employees stock ownership in the company. He then expanded his pharmaceutical operations into Russia. At the time, in an interview with the *Los Angeles Times*, I called him "The Ross Perot of the Balkans."

But even the business world wasn't big enough to contain Milan's ambitions and optimism. Recognizing that Yugoslavia's backward Communist government was the greatest obstacle to the nation's economic growth, he set out to change that government, too, by introducing democratic and economic reforms to the land of his birth—first, by serving as prime minister of Yugoslavia while Slobodan Milosevic was president of the state of Serbia, and then by challenging Milosevic for the presidency of Serbia.

Sadly, as this book will relate, his efforts all too often went both unrecognized and unsupported by leaders of his own adopted country, the United States. Yet, even after being rebuffed by the American government and exiled from Yugoslavia by Milosevic, Milan continued to work tirelessly to help the Balkan people, jetting from Washington to Moscow to Paris to Geneva to help fashion an end to the violence in Bosnia and Kosovo. Ironically, in the end, he played a major, behind-the-scenes role at the Dayton Peace Conference, advising both Presidents Clinton and Milosevic on a final peace agreement.

I first met Milan in 1978, during Jerry Brown's reelection campaign, and have known him as a friend for over thirty-five years. He's a brilliant, hard-driving, phenomenally successful man, and like all of us he has his faults—he always plays close to the line and, sometimes, over the line. That being said, he's also been a very generous supporter of many noble causes, and is very loyal to his friends, among whom I consider myself lucky to be counted. And as *Prime Minister for Peace* covers in captivating detail, it is in no small part because of Milan's hard work and hard-charging personality—both as prime minister of Yugo-slavia and as concerned observer from afar—that democratic reforms came to Serbia at last.

PROLOGUE

Kevin C. Murphy

Under a blood orange sky, as the Belgrade streets emptied for the dinner hour and the setting sun cast ominous shadows across the ancient city below, Milan Panic took a sip of wine and nervously glanced over at the ranting, desperate madman beside him. Once again, he wondered ruefully how he had found himself in this strange situation.

As a young man, Milan had risked it all for freedom—fighting the Nazis and, later, defecting from his Communist homeland to seek out a better life. Starting with nothing but the same cast-iron will that had made him a cycling champion in Yugoslavia, he had amassed an enviable fortune in his new home of California. He had become rich, well-respected, well-connected—businessmen looked up to him and politicians sought out his advice. In so many ways, he had achieved the American Dream that he had pined for from afar as a boy.

And yet, at an age when many men would be content to slow down, relax, and rest on the laurels of success, here he was on a chilly veranda back in Belgrade, thousands of miles away from the nourishing California sun, staring at an increasingly drunk, depressed, and unhinged Slobodan Milosevic. How had it come to this?

There were excellent reasons, of course. If glory was what motivated Panic—it wasn't, not anymore—he could take pride in being only the second American, after Golda Meir, to serve as prime minister of a foreign country. Soon he would become only the third Californian, after Richard Nixon and Ronald Reagan, to speak before the United Nations General Assembly. He would be hailed as the harbinger of freedom, prosperity, and better times by tens of thousands of his countrymen, and the man who would finally unseat the dictator of Serbia in a democratic election. He would serve as an advisor to presidents, including U.S. president Bill Clinton, on the pathway to peace.

But Milan wasn't in it for glory or admiration. He had already achieved all that, in spades. He had left his business and palatial Pasadena home behind because he wanted to make a difference for Yugoslavia—to help the land of his birth emerge from Communism, to bring that same vision of liberty and prosperity that had sustained him, all those years ago in the library, back to his original home. Most of all, he wanted to end the killing. Ever since his time as a young partisan in World War II, Milan had loathed the sort of carnage and violence now unfolding across the Balkans. Nothing, he thought, was more important than peace.

Still, Milan winced, he had not expected this. He was a self-made millionaire many times over, and no man reaches that rarified stratum of entrepreneurial success by being naïve. But here the rules were different. Nothing in California had prepared him for the ancient enmities, festering slights, and byzantine bureaucratic corridors of Belgrade.

Milan was accustomed to dealing with businessmen, who negotiated tough but shared a desire for profit. Now, he spent endless hours dealing with what seemed to him fundamentally irrational people: ruthlessly ambitious politicians who trafficked and fed on fear, grievance, and ethnic hatred. Condescending diplomats whose cleverness far exceeded their wisdom. Officious and often duplicitous government officials who made their keep navigating an arcane web of Balkan bureaucracy.

And at the center of this web sat the Spider—the tyrant himself, Serbian president Slobodan Milosevic—who both fueled, and was engorged by, the ancient grievances haunting this land. This was the man now standing next to him, his manner dangerously erratic, his features both feverish and dulled by whiskey.

Milan had been warned—most notably by his close friend and confidante, former ambassador to Yugoslavia Jack Scanlan—that Milosevic was a deeply disturbed and dangerous individual, that he was crazy like a fox, and that he would likely prove the undoing of all Milan hoped to achieve for his former homeland. But Milan had believed, with all the confidence and force of personality that had paved his way to success for so many years, that he could get through to Milosevic, and encourage him to do what was clearly best for their shared nation: step down.

That effort is what had brought the two men to this veranda, overlooking a darkening Belgrade. That effort Milan had just poured his heart and soul into, not minutes before. But even the thought of stepping down seemed to send Slobodan Milosevic, a sad and desperate man on the best of days, into a paroxysm of rage, grief, and loathing. And this time, it was worse than ever. When Milan looked over at his rival once again, his blood curdled. Milosevic, his eyes wild with drink and despair, now brandished a revolver.

For Serbs around the world, Milan Panic's life is a well-known success story. To those unfamiliar with his biography, it reads like something out of a Horatio Alger novel. A champion cyclist who fled from Communist Yugoslavia in 1955, Panic arrived in America with less than two hundred dollars in his pocket. Three years later, he founded a company with a grandiose name, International Chemical & Nuclear Corporation, and even grander ambitions. Over the course of decades, through determination, unwavering self-confidence, and a relentless will to succeed, Panic turned that company into ICN Pharmaceuticals, Inc., a multibillion-dollar company listed on the New York Stock Exchange. In the process, he became a millionaire many times over.

In many ways, Panic's determined rise from almost penniless obscurity to wealth and renown is the embodiment of what is often called the American Dream: Propelled only by his own immense energy and burning ambition, the new arrival to American shores managed to achieve vast success merely by taking advantage of opportunities and working hard day in and day out. For Panic, success in the United States was no accident: This is what the promise of America had always been, and why he had risked so much to leave his native Yugoslavia and come to the United States in the first place.

Animated by his secular faith in American ideals of liberty, democracy, and opportunity, Panic wanted nothing more than to be an American, and when he arrived in 1956, he broke with his past and embraced his new home. He renounced his Yugoslavian citizenship and became a naturalized American. He refused to have anything to do with Serbia. He did not speak his native language or attend the Serbian church. For decades, as his business and reputation grew in California and across the United States, Panic looked only westward.

But in the early 1990s, as the Cold War finally thawed, the grip of Communism loosened, and the world began to anticipate a new democratic spring in Eastern Europe, Panic's interest turned back to the nation of his youth. And when Yugoslavia began to disintegrate in the early 1990s, Panic felt he needed to help the country of his birth and reverse the destructive course on which that country's ethnic leaders were headed.

Just as important, Panic felt this was the chance to bring back to Yugoslavia the same political and economic ideals that had paved the way for his own success. "I believe the world one day will become like America," Panic said upon receiving the Ellis Island Medal of Honor in 1986. "To be an immigrant and to be accepted and recognized means that I am a part of a tremendous vision of a future where people will live like immigrants in the whole world and nobody will care where others come from as long as they contribute something to the life of everyone else." This was the vision Panic hoped to instill in his former country. And who better to shepherd Yugoslavia through a tough transition and uncertain future than the prodigal son, now returned from the United States with a critical understanding of the West's political and economic strengths?

At first, Panic's goals in Yugoslavia were primarily economic. In the early 1990s, when he returned to Yugoslavia to buy and renovate a struggling state-owned pharmaceutical factory, he rented for his offices the entire fifteenth floor of the former headquarters of the Yugoslav Communist party. Panic relished the panoramic view from his new suite, below the confluence of the Danube and the Sava Rivers and near a promontory atop of which stands the ruins of an ancient fortress. But the irony of the situation appealed to him even more. Sitting in the richly appointed office of the late Marshal Tito, the very man whose policies had forced him to flee his homeland in 1955, he would quip with a smile, "Not bad for a poor little immigrant, eh?"

As Panic entered the political arena in Yugoslavia, however, he soon discovered that steering his former homeland's transition from Communism to Democracy would be much more challenging and complicated than simply taking Tito's office for his own. Soon, Panic's love of country and fervent belief in the United States' guiding ideals would take him on an almost surreal journey. One day he was a wealthy California businessman, well connected to political power players at both the state and national levels; the next, he was prime minister of a chaotic and troubled nation at war with its neighbors, a pariah in the international community. Soon he would learn a good deal more about both of his home countries.

Some called him a fool. His own government distrusted him. The Washington politicians who had welcomed his contributions to their political campaigns and happily dined at his California table ignored him. But Panic nevertheless believed, with all the stubbornness of a man who had willed himself to success despite the odds, that he could make a difference. He had a plan: to stop the war that had set neighbor against neighbor, to recognize the independence of all former Yugoslav republics and have them incorporated into the European Union, and to turn the country's energies toward economic reconstruction. He knew this would be a heavier lift than anything the business world had prepared him for. But he still believed there was a "small chance" that he could do some good, and that he could enrich his entire nation by helping it to embrace the same ideals that had paved his way to prosperity. It was, he said, not a matter of proving himself to others. "If there was one person I would have liked to have impressed," he once said, "that would be my mother. But she's dead."

Initially, it did not turn out the way Panic hoped. But today, thanks in large part to his efforts, there is a free and democratic Serbia. If the world had listened to Panic in 1992, the bloody era of violence that defined the Balkans of the 1990s might well have been avoided. Slobodan Milosevic, the architect of so many of the former Yugoslavia's travails, could have been deposed. Kosovo might never have been plunged into ethnic cleansing. Srebrenica might be remembered for its legendary silver mines, rather than as the site of the worst massacre in Europe since World War II.

The missed opportunity of Milan Panic's tenure as prime minister of Yugoslavia is tragic—all the more so because his vision for democracy and economic prosperity was undone by Machiavellian politics, by human and diplomatic error, by ancient antagonisms that could not be subdued, and by the wily machinations of an unstable dictator, Slobodan Milosevic. Nonetheless and even in failure, Milan Panic fought an important fight in his brief foray into Yugoslavian politics. This is his story.

I

A BALKAN YOUTH

I will never forget Autokomanda Square. As I entered it in the fading light of a crisp December afternoon, a ghostly pall hung in the air. All around me, blank-faced people scurried about, intently staring at the snow beneath their feet and fearful of making eye contact with the horror that was right above them. Few people lingered, as any show of sympathy or anger could mean they would be next. I also looked away, but the grim images above my head floated in my mind's eye. My heart fluttered as I shuffled through the snow.

From Belgrade's ornamental lampposts, just above me—a blond, frightened, and angry fourteen-year-old boy—dozens of twisted and lifeless bodies hung like pendulums, swinging monotonously in the win-ter breeze. Some bodies drooped so low that their feet and ankles slapped against the windshields of passing streetcars. Above the nooses were dark, bloated faces, contorted forever into a horrifying rictus by the agonies and indignities of execution.

This grotesque carnival of death right in the center of town, and the war and occupation that had precipitated it, would have lasting effects on me. For the rest of my life, in the United States and upon my eventual return to Yugoslavia, my actions would be informed by the lessons I absorbed in my youth, as a boy becoming a man in a world of poverty, horror, deprivation, and war.

As the corpses in Autokomanda Square swayed obscenely to and fro, the sky grew darker—so much so that I felt an extraordinary relief when I reached the warmth of home. I sputtered as I told my mother what I had just seen. "Shhh, shhh," she said, putting her arm around me. "I know."

Everyone knew. The public executions by the Nazi occupiers, and the bodies that remained afterward, were frightening in their power and menace. "I want to join the people who are fighting against the Nazis," I said suddenly. In fact, the idea of joining the partisans had been percolating in my mind for weeks. She was still hugging me but I could feel her arms go rigid. "You are going to go to war? What is wrong with you? You know I love you but you are not ready. You are too young," she said. "When it thunders you still come to my bed."

I stiffened. "This is not a matter of young and old," I said. "It is a matter of right and wrong." Becoming agitated, my mother scolded me, "You can't go into the woods. They don't accept children, for God's sake." She was close to tears, but I knew she would not cry. My mother never cried. "I just wanted you to know," I said. "Shhh, Milan. You must not. Please." Her attitude was more than just disapproval—it was horror.

Fourteen was young, and I knew it. But many young men had gone to fight the Nazis. They simply vanished from the neighborhood, and the whispers began. They had "gone into the woods"—a euphemism for joining the guerrillas. In fact, many of my cousins and other relatives had already joined the partisans. In their occasional visits to my home, they urged me to come aboard. But going into the woods was one thing. Disobeying my mother—my rock and the most important person in my life—was something else altogether.

I would not have been the first Panic to take up arms in defense of my country. While I knew very little about my father, and even less about my grandfather, I knew plenty about their wars. While other countries inform their political culture with hopeful events, in Serbia the worse the calamity, the greater its social and cultural resonance. My grandfather, Stevan, had fought in the 1877–1878 war of independence against Turkey. My father, Spasoje, meanwhile, toiled first against the Turks in the Balkan War of 1912 and then again a year later in the Second Balkan War. Both then fought the Austrians and the Germans in World War I and, in 1915, marched with the defeated Serbian army across the Balkans to the Greek island of Corfu.

This martial lineage was not the only responsibility bequeathed to me. I was born into a family that belonged to an emerging urban class—

a comfortable, literate household of deeply patriotic parents who strongly believed they had a responsibility to play an active role in society. After the war against Turkey, grandfather Stevan had established a clothing business in the fashionable part of Belgrade in the 1880s. My father, Spasoje, completed the local high school before going to Vienna to study law. Upon his return, he married my mother, Zora Krunic, a high school graduate—rare in those days—who loved books, theater, and cafe society life.

When Stevan and Spasoje returned to Belgrade with the victorious Serbian army in 1918, my grandfather was a shadow of his former self and died soon afterward. But my father, full of enthusiasm for the new Yugoslav state, took a job in the Ministry of Interior and was appointed prefect in the Foca area of eastern Bosnia. It was a sensitive appointment, for Foca, on the Drina River, was predominantly Muslim. Now, for the first time in more than five centuries, the Foca Muslims were being ruled by Serbian leaders.

As prefect, my father was the top government official in Foca. A photograph taken at the time shows a stern-looking man with a long curly mustache and the uniform of a Balkan government official, a ceremonial saber attached to his side. He undoubtedly regarded the assignment in the gloomy mountainous region as a temporary one, because he never brought his wife and two teenage daughters to join him. Yet, he stayed in Foca for more than ten years and returned to Belgrade only two years before his death from a heart attack in 1932.

My birth on December 20, 1929, was one of the more joyful moments of my father's final years, as boys were highly prized in Serbian families. We lived in a detached house with a garden near Slavija, which in those days was at the edge of Belgrade's city limits. Sheep grazed in the fields behind my home. Only three miles away, Belgrade's city center, with its beautiful architecture and its markets full of spices and exotic enticements, seemed like another world.

A self-assertive scrapper from an early age, I was adored and doted upon by my two older sisters and my first cousin, a de facto third sister, who was adopted by the family after the death of her parents. Nor could I do any wrong in my mother's eyes. Widowed and left with a meager pension and some savings, my mother devoted her life to her children. She told me tales from Serb mythology about Prince Marko, the medieval hero whose horse had wings and spoke in a human voice to his master. This fearless prince fought evil invaders and killed dragons and monsters. I could become another Marko, she said. In fact, she constantly reminded me, I could become anything I wanted.

Photographs of my mother reveal her hard-worn features, indicative of the unyielding strength and emotional resilience that she conveyed to her children. One of my favorite photos of my mother shows her wearing a long coat and a dark hat angled down on her head and partially shading her face. I am holding her hand, my hair bleached by the sun. My mother was an imposing figure. She demanded much from me, but she also reinforced my natural optimism and self-confidence, and she gave me a sense of entitlement and adoration that never diminished.

To save money after my father's death, Zora moved to a smaller house far from the downtown area in the district of Vozdovac, Belgrade's most distant suburb. There, I attended a new elementary school, where I excelled in geography. I loved to pore over maps and read the life stories of Nikola Tesla and Michael Pupin, poor Serbian boys who went to America and became great inventors. It was then that my life-long fascination with the United States began. That land, far across the sea, became in my young mind the "land of opportunity." Years later, I would work to generously support U.S. overseas libraries, so that other young children around the world could have the same opportunity I had to learn more about, and become inspired by, the United States.

Delving through these books, I became particularly enthralled by a city in California called Pasadena, home to the California Institute of Technology. There, scientists were unraveling the mysteries of the universe. Pasadena became a lodestar of sorts for me—as a boy, I vowed to go to Caltech and become a professor. Already at the age of ten or eleven, I had assembled a small laboratory in my room to conduct experiments. While most of my classmates hated math, I found it gratifying, even beautiful. In algebra there were always clear answers. This innate faith in rationality and early love of science served to reinforce my belief, evidenced often later in life, that any problem could be solved with a reasoned and well-calibrated approach.

But at that very moment, reason and calibration were failing in the halls of diplomacy. Yugoslavia had initially hoped to remain neutral in the growing European conflict. But throughout the winter of 1940, the noose around my country's neck began to tighten. As Hitler's blitzkrieg inexorably stormed across Europe and concerted military opposition to Germany faltered at every turn, the diplomatic choices facing the other nations on the continent dwindled down to one: acquiescence or destruction. As such, Romania and Hungary joined the Axis alliance, and Bulgaria came on board in March 1941.

Hitler, who needed Yugoslavia as a conduit for transporting war materiel for the imminent invasion of Greece, summoned Yugoslav officials to his mountain retreat at Berchtesgaden. There, Hitler offered both carrots and sticks to Yugoslavia's regent Prince Paul. The Salonika territory of Greece could be annexed to Yugoslavia as a spoil of war, Hitler suggested. Or there could be terrible consequences for the entire country, if German demands were not acceded to. Unable to resist German pressure, the Yugoslav government accepted the offer and in the process kept much of her neutrality sacrosanct—no German troops would be allowed in Yugoslavia, and only war materiel could be transported across the country.

In hindsight, this was quite a diplomatic achievement, especially given Prince Paul's poor bargaining position and Hitler's then-overwhelming power on the European continent. But the Yugoslav people were outraged by the agreement. Students poured into the streets protesting the announcement. In the early hours of March 27, Prince Paul was deposed by General Dusan Simovic, the head of Yugoslavia's air force. It was a true people's revolution. As the veteran British journalist Richard West noted in his book *Tito and the Rise and Fall of Yugoslavia*, "common sense, caution and instinct for self-preservation were all on the side of accepting the pact; but these were not Serbian characteristics."

Angered by Yugoslavia's *volte-face* (at first he thought reports of the coup were a joke), Hitler ordered his troops to cauterize the Serbian ulcer. This was not simply war on Hitler's mind: He wanted to exact a swift and terrible retribution for disloyalty. In Belgrade, meanwhile, a strange calm had come over the city in the nine days since the coup d'état, as though Yugoslavia's precarious political situation had simply and magically been resolved. Few were anticipating or preparing for war. Even fewer were expecting how quickly a rather ordinary spring morning, Palm Sunday, would be turned into a day of unspeakable horror.

Early that fateful morning, April 6, 1941, Belgrade's streets teemed with families on the way to church or shopping in the city's markets. Just after 7:00 a.m., the first German Luftwaffe planes were spotted over the city—I remember sighting them from my home in the suburbs. The Stuka dive-bombers did not discriminate between civilian and military targets. Day and night, they bombed the defenseless city— military airports, antiaircraft positions, churches, hospitals, and even the National Library. More than seventeen thousand people were killed in the maelstrom, and a good portion of Belgrade was flattened by the Nazi barrage. Meanwhile, along the Austrian and Bulgarian frontiers, German troops poured across the nation's borders, overwhelming Yugoslavia's ill-prepared army.

Only three weeks later, swastikas fluttered over the National Theater. Banks collapsed. Schools closed down. For me, childhood was over. Under Italian and German auspices, a tiny, fascist movement, the Ustase, established an independent Croatian republic in Zagreb and then unleashed a wave of genocidal savagery on Serbs and Muslims. Even the hardened German troops were horrified by the atrocities of the Croats against their fellow Slavs. A much misunderstood part of the history of Yugoslavia, the excesses of the Ustase regime would be responsible for much of the animosity and suspicion that I would confront five decades later.

In the winter of 1941, one of the coldest on record, my family and I struggled to survive. I first collected firewood around the neighborhood. Later, I began vandalizing picket fences at night to help my family stay warm. But still we were forced to sleep huddled together in one room, close to the stove. Short of money, my mother would have to sell her prized personal possessions. When she returned home, she was holding a bag of groceries in each hand. My mother offered no explanation. I later learned about the incident from my sisters. My mother was a saint. Years later, when she was living in a wing of my Pasadena mansion, I once discovered that the cupboards of her kitchen were not fully stocked. "I never want to see this again," I told my staff angrily. "These cupboards must always be full."

The fierce deprivation of the war years bred in me an unerring instinct for survival and further honed my strong sense of initiative. With Belgrade in ruins and the country in disarray, I would have to find a way to provide for my family, for no one else would. And in the weeks after the German occupation of Yugoslavia, I sprang into action.

The most immediate need was for food. So I ventured to the local library, already one of my favorite haunts, and began to pore through books on how to grow vegetables. Soon a fertile garden began to take root behind my house—potatoes, tomatoes, cantaloupes, onions. With my pick, rake, and shovel, I would venture out each morning to till the land. I became so committed to my "farm" that I would wake up in the middle of the night and sit outside waiting for the sun to rise so I could get to work. Hungry Serbs came from all over to buy my potatoes, onions, string beans, corn, tomatoes, even watermelons and canta-loupes. In short time, I had four to five acres of land blooming and no one in the neighborhood was going hungry.

Soon, however, I began to see a problem. My family and I were not getting enough protein in our diet. Back to the library I went, where I discovered that rabbits were both an excellent source of protein and reproduced quickly. I started with two and soon had two hundred rab-bits for sale. I then began to raise chickens for their eggs, as well as goats and pigs.

But my success at farming notwithstanding, the war was never a happy time for me. The brutal executions at Autokomanda Square in particular changed everything. No longer was it enough to simply feed my family—I wanted to help liberate my country.

I had been deliberating for a while about joining the partisans. On the Serbo-Croatian service of the BBC, which I would try to listen to on my tiny radio, I heard the voice of Winston Churchill. His words cap-tured my imagination and stayed with me forever. Churchill knew how to fight evil, and he was totally determined to win. He arguably inspired me more than anyone else. He made me want to join the fight. In the early winter of 1943, shortwave broadcasts were talking about an immi-nent invasion of western Europe and Germany's military setbacks on the Russian front. The time was now! At school I discreetly asked an older student how one would get in contact with the underground. "Go to the Cafe Kumorda," the older student said. "Look for a waiter who walks with a limp, and tell him Misha has sent you."

And so I walked in face-freezing weather to the cafe, constantly looking over my shoulder to make sure I wasn't being followed. I en-tered wincing and a bit apprehensive. The cafe was full of smoke. Old men sat with cups of Turkish coffee, playing chess. I tried to remain serene as I approached the man in an apron behind the zinc bar. He was a broad-featured man with hairy fingers, probably in his fifties. "How old are you, son?" he gruffly asked. "Sixteen," I blurted out. Then, softly, I added, "Misha sent me." The man looked at me for a moment, and then said, "Go to the back and take out the trash! Follow me, I'll show you." Inside the gloomy storage room, I was asked a series of questions and was then instructed to show up the next day at the basement entrance to a nearby house. I left by the back door.

I had an entire day to prepare. I grabbed an extra pair of woolen socks, heavy knitted mittens, and a sweater and hid them in the back-yard shed. Next morning, I carefully tucked a note under my dear mother's pillow. I then wrapped a chunk of corn bread in a handker-chief and stashed it in the pocket of my coat. I picked up my parcel from the shed, rushed to the Kumorda cafe, crossed the street, and entered the dark basement. It was filled with the stench of wet boots and sodden clothes; the shadowy darkness seemed to make the odor even more pungent. I saw several men waiting, some young and others not so young. From the whispered tones and the gestures of the men, it was clear they, too, were going to the woods.

The bartender from the day before soon arrived and addressed them as comrades. They all looked at a map as his hairy fingers tapped a hillside village on the other side of the Avala Mountain, where we would be met by the partisans. Split into groups of five, we were told to make our way separately along a route he traced. Trudging through the pine forests, I rejoiced in the excitement of entering the clandestine world of the partisans. Like generations of Serbians before me, I was heading off to war. And like generations of Serbians before me, I would be forever changed by the experience.

The war years in Yugoslavia were like few others on the European continent. While other countries suffered in humiliation under the tyr-anny of Nazi rule, the Yugoslavia countryside became a war zone. We local partisans waged more than three years of bloody, brutal conflict with our Nazi occupiers—and with each other. Today, the partisans of Yugoslavia are frequently romanticized by historians, credited with bog-ging down several German divisions in a brutal guerrilla war. Yet the divided partisan armies of Yugoslavia often shed as much of each oth-er's blood as they did of their Nazi occupiers'. Even as they battled the

Germans, Tito's Communist forces and the royalist Chetnik partisans frequently waged a virtual civil war to determine who would rule the postwar Yugoslavia.

I was first assigned to a demolition squad blowing up railway lines and disrupting German communications along the train tracks linking Belgrade and Bucharest. There, my story almost ended early: In a desire to see my handiwork firsthand, I idled after setting one of my first explosions. Unaware of the true force of the blast, I was almost killed in the tumult as rocks from the railroad pelted me in the face. As time went on, however, my team and I became virtual demolition experts. It would take the Germans about two to three hours to repair the tracks— by then, we would be far away, doing more damage.

As partisans, my comrades and I lived a peripatetic existence. We were loosely organized in a cell in the Vojvodina region of Serbia. We hid in forests and abandoned barns and sheds during the day, or did our best to melt into our surroundings posing as civilians. Nobody had any serious military training, so we improvised. In the eyes of many of my compatriots, the German soldiers we captured were not human. They were the same twisted individuals who had willingly gunned down women and children. Not touched personally by tragedy, I would urge my fellow partisans toward mercy for our captives. "If we execute them," I pleaded, "we are no better than the Nazis." But men bent on revenge had little time for human rights, and I soon became horrified by the indiscriminate killing on both sides.

Few events would have a more significant impact on me than an incident near the end of the war, after the Soviet Army had already entered the country. The Russians forced hundreds of captured German soldiers into a shallow trench. Then they simply plowed over them with a tank, back and forth, until they were all dead. I watched in abject horror, and for the rest of my life I recoiled at the very idea of killing. Decades later, I still recall this experience as the exact moment when I became a pacifist.

As that atrocity indicated, the tide had turned decisively against the Germans by the end of 1944, and Josip Tito, the head of the partisans, began preparing for postwar contingencies. That summer, the Yugoslav Army was formally established and I was assigned to the Forty-Second Macedonian Brigade. I was made regimental courier and given a bicycle. I was a sparrow-weight boy who looked younger than my age, which made me perfectly suited for courier duty along a broad front in northern Yugoslavia. A few months later, in October 1944, Soviet soldiers crossed the Danube and the liberation of Yugoslavia was under way. Great jubilation ensued, and my buddies and I downed bottles of vodka and danced in celebration. Within a matter of days Belgrade was liberated as well. Now working as a courier under Russian command, I crisscrossed western Yugoslavia as my unit followed the Germans retreating toward the Austrian border.

It was during this time that I got my first taste of real combat. While the Soviets had proceeded to Belgrade, the partisans were given responsibility for cutting off the retreat of German soldiers—but we were no match for the experienced German troops. Even in full retreat, they were able to unleash frightening levels of violence. Near Srem, I manned a machine gun in battle with the Nazis, who considerably outnumbered us. I remember falling apart under the stress of combat, actually crying as bullets whizzed past me. I was convinced I was going to die. In the end, my unit was spared when German troops broke off the battle and continued their retreat—but this terrifying episode was a further reminder to me that I never wanted any part of military combat.

As the Germans retreated across Yugoslavia, the guerrilla army was further being transformed into a regular army, and I was noticed by General Zdenko Ulepic, a Croatian graduate of Moscow's Air Force Academy who was already a fast mover in the military hierarchy. Ulepic was impressed by my energy and efficiency and made me his personal aide. After the war's end, the general was assigned to the Air Force headquarters in Zagreb and took me along. As a personal aide to a senior general at only sixteen years old, I was in a position of considerable authority. I was in charge of the general's schedule and security, and had the right to commandeer a vehicle or demand special privileges.

Occasionally, so much power in the hands of an adolescent went to my head. One day, I went to the officers' club to get a haircut. Seeing some other officers being shaved, I sternly demanded one as well. The elderly barber looked at my smooth face with its faint traces of hair and began to chuckle. "There's nothing to shave," he said. The room exploded with laughter. My face went red and I jumped up. "Are you disobeying an order?" I shouted. "I'll have you court-martialed." The barber complied. It was my first experience in wielding authority, and it impressed many in the room—including the editor of a local news-paper. The next day, my picture was in the paper, next to an editorial reading "How to Demand Authority."

Only days after the war ended across Europe, Ulepic took his staff to a beach on the Sava River outside Zagreb to cool off on a hot, muggy summer day. There, the general broached the idea of making a career out of the military. "Go back to school, Milan," said Ulepic. "Then you can go to the military academy. I'll make sure you are accepted." It was tempting advice, but over the past two years I had seen and done enough to convince me that the military was not for me. I did go back to school, but my military career was over.

As I returned to Belgrade to resume my studies, my childhood, for all intents and purposes, was a distant memory. Dressed in my military tunic, a badge of honor in postwar Belgrade, I felt far older than the fourteen-year-old boy who had trudged off to war. After running a step ahead of death for more than a year, I had become a man and a survivor. Despite my innate optimism, the experience instilled in me a life-long sense of caution and reserve in the face of threatening or bullying behavior. At the same time, the constant fear of death gave me a desire to make every day count—to never rest in pursuit of my goals. I had always been driven in the past, but now I felt an almost pathological desire to succeed in the future.

Around me, Yugoslavia was undergoing extraordinary and painful change as well. The country was in tatters. People were poor and hun-gry, and children ran through the streets without shoes. Houses lacked central heating, and staples such as milk, lard, and cheese were ra-tioned. The main source of protein came in the shape of powdered eggs, promptly dubbed "Truman eggs" since they were supplied by the United States. Despite all of this, there was a sense of optimism in the air. People believed that things would turn around. And much of this was due to Josip Broz Tito, the former partisan who became the leader of Yugoslavia in the postwar years.

Many today denigrate Tito and portray Communism in Yugoslavia as an accident of history, and certainly Tito was ambitious, cynical, enor-mously self-confident, and driven to succeed. But unlike many of his countrymen, he abhorred ethnic divisions and tribalism. His new Yugo-slavia was to be based on his concept of "brotherhood and unity," in which Yugoslavians of decency and goodwill from across all ethnic communities would come together to forge a civilized, coherent nation. Well before he came to power, Tito's politics found resonance among the educated classes, particularly after the nation's new leaders embarked on sweeping reforms to ensure equality, women's rights, and ethnic tolerance.

Though I would largely reject Communism, I was forever changed by Tito's vision of "one Yugoslavia"—a land united in pursuit of common goals. When I returned to govern Yugoslavia in 1992, it was this vision of an integrated and economically sustainable country—comprised of a union of diverse states not unlike America—that would define much of my political thinking.

Like many, however, I quickly soured on Communism itself. While briefly inspired by the prospect of building a blissful utopia in southeastern Europe, the wild expectations, the sense that the new system would instantly transform people's lives for the better, gave way to sobering second thoughts. For it soon happened that the new social order was not much different from the previous one. Contrary to both the theory and the rhetoric, it had its own elite, a compact new group formed from those who had taken part in the Communist-led resistance, and who were now determined to secure and expand their own power and privilege.

Having been a partisan, I could have joined the Communist Party, gone into politics, and enjoyed a relatively rich and comfortable life as a party apparatchik. But that was not my dream. My life-long contrarian streak grew more developed under Communism. I recoiled at the collectivist nature of the Communist system, with its all-embracing paternalism backed by secret police. Where was the sense of personal initiative or entrepreneurship? How could anyone reach their potential in a system that discouraged creativity and celebrated conformity? "Sparks live in the rock, only blows find them there" was a Serb proverb that came to define my worldview.

For all the rhetoric of comradeship and collectivism going around Tito's Yugoslavia at the time, I was a natural loner. I preferred to go my own way. Where other boys loved team activities such as soccer and basketball, my favorite sports were solitary ones, such as skiing, swimming, and biking. My continued pursuit of cycling—the wartime job that would soon become my own personal instrument of liberation—speaks, I think, to my personality. Cycling is neither the most romantic of sports, nor the most enjoyable. It's a painful activity that tests mental toughness and resilience as much as physical strength. But a sport that relied foremost on a contest of will is one that I was well-suited for. Each day, I would jump on my bike and head out by myself to train, keeping track of my time and my stamina and testing the outer limits of my endurance. Within a year, I was a junior champion in the thousand-meter sprint.

Cycling brought me a focus I did not then enjoy in my studies. In 1952, I enrolled at the medical school of the University of Belgrade. This was a prestigious honor, as the university was considered among the best in the country—but after two years, I came to the realization that a medical career was not for me. "I can't take it," I told the dean of the school. Whether it interfered with my optimistic sense of the world or brought back painful memories of the war, something about being surrounded by sick and dying people was more than I could bear.

Making matters worse for me, under Communism young people were assigned their future profession by the government, which decided exactly how many engineers, doctors, and teachers the country needed. My lot, it was decreed, was dentistry. Clearly, I did not want to spend my life drilling teeth and filling cavities—it fit neither my goals nor my temperament. Instead, I wanted to go to America and become another Tesla or Oppenheimer or Fermi. I was determined to go to Pasadena, and to Caltech.

During my time in medical school, I continued to pursue my cycling career, which gave me important opportunities to travel abroad. By 1952, I was a member of Yugoslavia's Olympic cycling team, and traveled to Helsinki and Germany for international tournaments. Daily exercises—sprinting, long-distance endurance, strategy—became my preoccupation. I possessed a will to excel, and my drive and tenacity helped to make me a champion in the thousand meters and place me among the five top racers in the nation.

This international travel encouraged me to begin thinking more seriously about defection. Unlike many of my fellow countrymen, I had the opportunity to compare the richer and more abundant life of the West with the poverty and blunted ambitions of my life in Yugoslavia. I saw that we were living in a world without freedom, a single-directed world. I started to be afraid of it. But it would not be easy to escape. While traveling overseas, Yugoslav sportsmen were chaperoned by security officials. They were only allowed to go out in pairs and were never to meet with strangers. If the authorities had information that anyone was contemplating defection, passports would be taken on the tarmac and individuals immediately sent home. Nonetheless, by the summer of next year, I had made up my mind and felt the need to brace my mother. "I've been thinking," I whispered to her one evening. "What would you say if I decided to stay in the West?"

"I knew you were thinking about it," my mother replied. "I could feel it. I can see you aren't happy." "Mom, I would not be coming back. I want to go to America." "America, America," she said quietly. "Go. Don't worry about me, please." This may have been the toughest moment of my life. I had a plan. But I still did not want to leave my mother.

But, just then, another woman reentered my life. I had first met Jelica Narandzic in grammar school. At the tender age of eight, before all the bruising memories of the occupation and war, we had held hands as we walked together to school. Later, we would date in high school, but eventually grew apart. And yet here she was again.

A dreamy art history student who resembled a young Elizabeth Taylor, Jelica was already married and had an infant son, Nicholas. But by the time she and I reunited, her marriage was on the rocks. After a short courtship our love was rekindled, and I asked her to marry me. She soon divorced her army captain husband and married me in Belgrade in December 1954. The wedding, however, threw a wrench into my defection plans. I could not leave without my new bride, and I faced the added challenge of helping bring her son to the West as well. But, to me, it was worth it—I was no longer interested in seeking a new life alone.

Like thousands who escaped from Communist Eastern Europe in the 1950s, Jelica and I carefully planned each step of our getaway. I was scheduled to participate in an international race in Maastricht, Holland, in August of 1955. Jelica obtained permission to accompany me, our infant son remaining with her grandmother as a guarantee that we would in fact in return. Once we were established in America, I believed that the Communist authorities would permit the child to join us. (I underestimated both their resolve and bureaucracy—it would ultimately take eight years to get Nick out of Yugoslavia.)

The Yugoslav national cycling team left Belgrade on August 1 for the Dutch tournament. During a stopover at Vienna, I told my colleagues I was not planning to return home. I stood up, departed the aircraft, and immediately requested political asylum. Jelica, meanwhile, arrived by train. Western newspapers, always happy to see the Iron Curtain fraying, described it as a "Dash to Freedom: Red Athlete Bicycles to Freedom." However, the politics of defection never much motivated me. It was not an act of defiance or political expression per se. I simply wanted to pursue my dreams, and America, the Land of Opportunity, would finally give me that chance.

But first, I had to prove that I merited political asylum. We were sent to a refugee camp in West Germany, assigned refugee numbers, and placed on the list of unfortunates awaiting resettlement. All of these refugees, waiting for precious entry visas, were suspended in limbo. Having forfeited everything—our careers, our possessions, our past lives—we were alone and friendless in a strange country, knowing neither the language nor the customs. What's more, we could also be sent back at any time.

When the time came, I was forced to appear in court and plead my case for asylum. My court-appointed lawyer advised me to remain quiet as he lobbied the judge. But I would have none of it and addressed the court regardless. First, I began (to the dismay of my legal counsel), I did not feel comfortable living among Germans; after all, they were the Serbs' natural enemies. I had fought German soldiers during the war, and Germany had destroyed my country twice in the past half century, in World Wars I and II.

At this point, my lawyer was apoplectic and begged me to stop, but I continued. "It is strange for me to sit here and be judged by you," I told the judge, "but I think you should know how I feel." But then I explained how, after only a few months in the country, I had already made German friends, found a job in construction, and had even been enrolled at the local university. In short, I concluded, getting to the point, my story was proof that it was possible to move beyond the prejudices of the past.

I was persuasive. Jelica and I were granted asylum and given German passports. For the first time in months, we could relax. We were not going to be sent back to Yugoslavia. Now the future was wide open.

And I well knew, after months and years of intensive training, how far and fast I could go when given an open road to push myself.

2

THE MAKING OF AN AMERICAN

While I was now able to stay in Germany, I still dreamed of that citadel of science and technology I'd read about in the library as a child—Pasadena, California. So Jelica and I applied for inclusion in a U.S. program that resettled refugees in America, and, in 1955, only a few months after my defection, we were accepted. Forty-eight hours after we arrived in New York, we boarded a train for the West Coast. For three days, we stared out the train windows, mesmerized by the vastness of the American landscape. In Yugoslavia, land was a finite concept. In the United States, it seemed to roll on forever.

All the while, the state I had dreamt of for so long slowly inched into view. And when I arrived, I was immediately enchanted. California in 1956 was booming—Americans were also flocking to the West Coast to take up jobs in the growing postwar economy. With its face toward the Pacific, the Golden State seemed far removed from the eternal conflicts of Europe. For most of the state's residents, there was little interest in the past. Theirs was the land of the future, and one that was building its own destiny. For me, the opportunity the idea of the West had always afforded—to invent a new identity from scratch, undisturbed by the past—was exactly what I wanted from my new home.

We were met in Los Angeles by my cousin Momo Stamenkovic, an older man who lived in Huntington Beach. He immediately offered us a roof over our heads. I had dreamt for so long about Caltech that, the first chance I got, I rushed to Pasadena, debating in my mind what I would say to the admissions officer during the bus ride over. I strolled around the campus, sizing up the old mansions on its perimeter. Eventually, I decided on the most direct approach and found my way to the admissions office. "I want to enroll," I told the shocked receptionist.

She took me to an office where two counselors spoke with me. They were friendly, but it was quickly clear to them that my English was simply inadequate. They talked with me for a while, then advised me against applying for now. I should take an English language course, they suggested, then try to apply next year. Dejected, I sat for hours on a bench outside the administration building, scorched by the broiling midday sun. My childhood dream, which had only recently seemed so close, now appeared to recede. Rebuffed by Caltech! I had never even imagined the possibility. For the first time in my life, I began to feel a sense of uncertainty, of limitation. And yet, I thought, they had a legitimate reason. Clearly I needed to learn English.

Unfortunately, Momo and his wife, who fancied herself a painter, preferred Serbo-Croatian. To me, trying to figure out the way things worked in America through a Serbian filter was excruciating—but I was the outlier in many ways. The majority of California's Serb community had come to the Golden State for many of the same reasons as we did. Fleeing the interminable Balkan wars, corruption, and oppression of their homeland, they found economic security and happiness in the New World. But many Serbian immigrants of the time also had a different relationship with their original homeland than we did—especially on Sundays, when, as they gathered in church, they were transformed. Conflating nationality, tradition, culture, and faith, the Serbian Orthodox Church provided many American Serbs with an outlet to their past. Women prepared Serbian food and gossiped. Men sipped wine or beer and talked about their children and relatives in the old country.

Cousin Momo belonged to a distinct group of the diaspora: the expatriates who were driven out of Yugoslavia by the Communists during World War II. They were far different from the immigrants that preceded them. Despite their gratitude to the United States for taking them in, they felt alienated from what they thought of as a soulless American society. They longed for the world of their youth. Most of all, however, they were vehemently anti-Communist. Momo himself was a former royalist army officer who could whip himself into a fury at even the very mention of Tito or Communism. He had enjoyed a good life before the war, when I was still a boy. I even remember Momo taking us for a spin around Belgrade in his shiny new car.

Life in Huntington Beach was altogether different. Momo had a small shop where he repaired washing machines. He was a melancholy working stiff who wore T-shirts and blue jeans and drove a jalopy. To me, he and his friends seemed inextricably attached to the glory days of their youth. From time to time they tried to recreate their past, leaving their shabby ethnic neighborhoods behind. They would meet for dinner at a fancy French restaurant, adorned in formal clothes, and tell the same anti-Communist jokes and complain about their bad luck. Life, as far as they were concerned, was all about luck. In the midst of their dashed hopes, they clung to the solace of family, tradition, and the rare night out.

I looked at this mind-set with disdain. "They carry their past strapped to their backs," I would say to my wife. For me, the past was like a bad dream; I had no interest in wallowing in it. I could not understand the sense of victimhood that animated so many of my Serbian refugee brethren. When Momo offered me a job in his shop, I declined. I told him I would rather work as a steelworker at Kaiser Steel plant in Fontana and make my own way. And so I did.

To me, freedom and opportunity are real concepts, not mere slogans. And it was up to me and me alone to make something of myself in my new home of California. Of course, freedom also took even more concrete forms as well. Perhaps the biggest highlight of my first year in California was my purchase of a 1936 Ford. Now I was no longer a pitied yokel, always trying to hitch a ride or take the bus to and fro. This was freedom!

In the meantime, I practiced English with locals at a neighborhood pharmacy. I was fascinated by its long counters, its revolving high stools, its vast array of merchandise, the strange tasting ice-cream sodas dished out by efficient soda jerks. I looked through paperback books on a rack near the front counter and perused the want ads in the newspapers. Most importantly—conceding to myself at last that Pasadena was not the only path forward in this new land of promise—I applied for admission to the University of Southern California, and was accepted.

After I received a promotion at Kaiser Steel, Jelica and I moved to Fontana, an industrial town north of Los Angeles, and plunged into American life with even greater ardor. After all the dislocations and uncertainties, and the humiliation of exile in Germany, our tiny rented apartment seemed like paradise. Some thought Fontana the dreariest part of southern California, but I loved it. Even the most mundane tasks were blissful, from shopping at the supermarket to simply puttering around my apartment, a free man.

"I knew from the first day that I would make it in America," I often tell my friends, and that is a true story. I love everything American—the culture, the language, the sense of opportunity. I told Jelica we should no longer speak our native tongue, eat Serbian food, or have anything to do with our past. I renounced my Yugoslavian citizenship and wanted to leave my past and start afresh as an American.

I found a second job as a lab assistant, and Jelica got a secretarial job. During the day I attended class and worked as a laboratory technician. At midnight, I checked in to my regular job at Kaiser where I was paid $1.25 per hour—at the time an excellent wage. My job was to take samples from the furnaces and analyze them; in between, I kept my nose stuck in a book.

The inherent difficulties of being a full-time student and holding down two jobs slowly began to take their toll. The commute between Fontana and Los Angeles was exhausting, and I would frequently show up to class barely able to stay awake. One professor became so concerned that he discreetly left $100 in an envelope for me, without an explanation. While I was not one to accept handouts, I was nonetheless happy for the much-needed cash, which helped me to put a two hundred-dollar down payment on a house in Fontana. The next year, our first child, Dawn, was born. She would be followed by a son, Milan Jr., and another daughter, Vivien.

Fortunately for me and my family, I soon came up with the idea of a successful moneymaking scheme, the first of many in my life. Radioactive isotopes were in high demand by the burgeoning number of research labs across the state. Drawing on my studies at the university and work in the lab, I realized I could produce these compounds and sell them to researchers at prices lower than what it cost to produce them in-house. I immediately began mixing chemical substances in the basement of my house and marketing them to research institutes and university labs. "Instead of making them yourself," I pitched, "why not buy them from me?"

I had keyed in on a potential source of income that was not all that far removed from my playtime as a child in Yugoslavia—instead of conducting science experiments in my bedroom laboratory, I was now producing chemical compounds in my California basement. But a small operation in my home was not going to make me rich, and so, in the fall of 1959, I decided to put out my own shingle and go into business for myself. With $200 in savings, I founded a company I ambitiously titled International Chemical and Nuclear Corporation (ICN). I then went to friends, colleagues, and former teachers for the additional start-up capital.

Among the academics who agreed to back me from early on was Roberts Smith, a biochemistry professor at the University of California, Los Angeles. Smith recalls, "Milan worked for a very good friend of mine, John Moffatt, at Calbiochem, then a small company manufacturing biochemicals. John called me and said this guy was starting a company and was I interested in helping him. I went to Milan's house where we shared a bottle of wine and discussed his idea. I was immediately impressed. He had thought through his business idea and had a plan to make it work."

ICN's first product was commercialized DNA for use by nucleic acid researchers. Unable to afford sophisticated equipment, I used an old washing machine as a centrifuge to extract the material from salmon sperm and snake venom. "From the outset, ICN was manufacturing the most advanced products in the most primitive conditions," Smith said. The business side of the little company was also a bit primitive. "When somebody asked about cash flow," Smith recalled, "Panic responded, 'What's cash flow?'" But I learned quickly. "A couple of years later, he was the master of cash flow."

A loner by nature, I became a loner in business. I trusted only a few close friends and kept my business ideas close to my vest. I was tough, brash, an indefatigable salesman with a jovial personality, successful because I understood intuitively the secret of business—when you are selling your products, you are also selling yourself. I know I have little patience for those who don't quickly grasp my ideas, but my employees also know I am unfailingly loyal to them if they are to me. Fred Andrea, who joined my company in 1963, once said, "The same people who hated Panic, loved Panic."

In any event, the 1960s and early 1970s were years of growth for ICN. When sales climbed, ICN became a public company. I then traded newly issued company stock for ownership of other small companies in the biochemical and pharmaceutical industries. As the company grew to the point where its shares were listed on the New York Stock Exchange, ICN began to live up to its name: It expanded internationally through acquiring companies in Europe and Latin America. The company became an industry leader in developing and manufacturing biochemicals, nucleic acids, and radioisotopes.

With ICN prospering, I fulfilled a longtime ambition in a slightly different fashion than I had originally intended—I bought a huge, Tudor-style mansion in Pasadena on a multiacre site near the Caltech campus. In fact, the mansion had caught my eye that first week in the United States, when I had rushed to Pasadena to enroll at Caltech. The three-story building has a proper wine cellar, a landscaped garden, a swimming pool and tennis court, a detached guesthouse, servants' quarters, and two huge garages.

Meanwhile, my acquisition spree increased ICN's profits to the point that I had enough money to fund original research. I recruited a staff of top scientists, charged them with developing new drugs, and built them a new research center on ten acres in Irvine, California, close to what is today the John Wayne Airport—which became the home for my corporate jet. But when costs of that lab and its occupants mounted, I moved the corporate headquarters and its entire staff from Pasadena to Irvine and stuffed the entire company into the laboratory buildings so I could keep a closer eye on expenditures.

Tired of commuting from Pasadena to Irvine, I bought a home on the bay in Newport Beach not far from the Irvine offices. But I have never parted with the Pasadena manor. This remains my psychological and physical anchor, the embodiment of my American Dream, the place where my children grew up and where the neighbors know me. I modernized the Pasadena mansion to my satisfaction, and then filled it with antiques; European paintings; and, in one niche, a full set of armor. I admit now that not all my purchases were wisely chosen. Once I returned from London with several tons of old Georgian silver and proudly invited my neighbor and friend Arthur Gilbert, a well-known collector, to review the purchases. "Milan," Gilbert chided me gently, "you have become a junk collector."

Even though I have become a wealthy businessman, I have always well remembered the days of hardship in Yugoslavia. And so I have always tried to remain sensitive to the plight of others, and to the call to service for which my family was known in the Old World. I believe in idealism and compassion, as well as the importance of doing good along with doing well. I was once approached by a New York physician who asked me to make a contribution toward inoculating Albanian children in the Serb-held province of Kosovo. "Shouldn't all the children be inoculated?" I wondered, and I prevailed. In the end, all 800,000 children in the impoverished province were inoculated, regardless of religion or ethnicity.

Largely for sentimental reasons, I started out as a Republican—the refugee support program that originally brought me to the United States had been sponsored by then Vice President Richard Nixon. But, like many, I was mesmerized by John F. Kennedy. Kennedy's New Frontier idealism, with its concern for education, civil rights, and the alleviation of poverty, touched me deeply. And Kennedy's liberal social views came, for me, to define America's necessary and indispensable role in the world.

While skiing in Aspen, Colorado, in 1964, I met Birch Bayh, the then Democratic senator from Indiana. We talked politics and became good friends. Through Bayh, I was introduced to other Democratic politicians on the national scene, including Lyndon Johnson, Jimmy Carter, and Bill Clinton, as well as California's then senator Alan Cranston, and its father and son governors, Pat and Jerry Brown. I served as finance chairman of Bayh's short-lived presidential bid in 1976 and became close to Carter, whom I admired for his moral courage. These political efforts were the logical outgrowth not just of my interest in service, but my extraordinary pride in being an American and the democratic ideals this wonderful nation has always espoused.

As I prospered, I enjoyed a life of increasing luxury. But tragedy struck, not once, but twice in 1976. First, my wife, Jelica, who had risked it all to leave Yugoslavia, who had traversed the ocean and continent with me, who had been there right alongside me as we carved out a new life in California, died after a long illness. Just months later, Junior, my son whom I deeply loved and who I thought would carry on my family business, was killed in an accident in Spain.

I was initially inconsolable—a wife and son gone. My daughter Dawn remembers, "My mother's death was traumatic enough but this pushed us all over the edge." It was nearly a year before I fully recovered. To numb the pain, there was work—always my narcotic of choice. As I told my old friend Roberts Smith, "The only way to get over it is to work harder. The harder you work the less you think about it."

And in 1977, there was plenty of that. Currency fluctuations, coupled with growing U.S. inflation, began to inflict huge losses on ICN's foreign sales. The price of ICN stock plummeted. Debts the company had incurred to finance acquisitions became burdensome. And as business periodicals began to report that ICN was on the verge of bankruptcy, a group of stockholders led by an old friend of mine, wealthy California rancher Lionel Steinberg, mounted a proxy battle for control of the company.

I fought back and won, but not without cost—ICN stock, once over $40 a share, dropped to only $2. To get rid of debt and save the company, I sold off subsidiaries and factories, abandoned the multistory corporate headquarters in Orange County, and moved to Covina, California, just west of Los Angeles, taking up space in one of the few remaining production facilities. Sales in 1979 were a mere $29 million—compared to $180 million the year before. Gone were all the accoutrements of my meteoric rise: my jet aircraft, my stretch limo, my driver and personal servants. Now I drove myself to work.

My climb back was fueled by hard work, as well as the development of new products and new drugs. From the early days at ICN, the search for antiviral and anticancer agents had been a key focus of the laboratory. In the early 1970s, a team of ICN scientists led by Dr. Roland K. Robins had discovered one of the first antiviral drugs, which they named ribavirin and would later market as Virazole. I still recall Robins's announcement at an ICN meeting. "Gentlemen," the doctor had said, "in 1929, Fleming discovered the first broad spectrum antibacterial drug which he named penicillin. Today, we are following in his footsteps with our own first broad-spectrum antiviral."

Unfortunately, the U.S. Food and Drug Administration was less enthusiastic. Mexican authorities approved the drug for treatment of viral respiratory infections and hepatitis C in 1974. Brazil followed later that same year. More than forty countries approved sale of the drug before ICN received FDA approval just to mount clinical tests in the United

States. Some of that testing was done on AIDS patients, 80 percent of them also suffering from hepatitis C. The preliminary results were encouraging. The drug appeared to slow progression of the HIV virus.

Thrilled by the promise of ribavirin, I began to talk publically about the possibility that the drug would prove an important tool in the battle against AIDS. My friend ICN director Steve Moses thought this was "Serbian enthusiasm getting ahead of American business," but I strongly believed this drug could play an important role in the fight against this terrible scourge, which was ravaging our state of California and killing so many before their time. But the FDA chairman then, Frank Young, dismissed ICN's findings. "We just don't believe this data," he said.

Frustrated, I called Young "a jerk." Our stock, which had been rising, plummeted once again. Dissident stockholders once more tried to depose me. And the Securities and Exchange Commission and the Justice Department mounted separate investigations aimed at determining whether I had profited from my promotion of the drug and the subsequent run-up in the stock price. To settle the issue and move on, the ICN board of directors agreed to pay a $600,000 fine. To this day, I regret this settlement. I should have never agreed to it. I had not committed any crime. But I took the advice of the lawyers, who said it's cheaper to pay the government than to continue to litigate. I should have never done it.

This sour experience only spurred me to pour more of my time and effort into ICN. In 1985, ICN quietly bought 10 percent of one of the world's largest pharmaceutical companies, Switzerland's Hoffman-La-Roche. When I offered to buy the rest, I was rejected. So I secured a $4 billion line of credit and began to proceed with a hostile takeover bid. But the Swiss resistance discouraged ICN's board of directors, who urged me to abandon the fight. When I agreed and sold my interest in the Swiss company, ICN still garnered a $100 million profit on the transaction.

The fall of the Berlin Wall and the collapse of the Soviet empire also intrigued me. I became mesmerized by the long-term potential of the Russian and Eastern European markets. At a time when many were unwilling to dabble in a region rising from five decades of Communism, I started by looking for opportunities—beginning in Yugoslavia, the country where I still had relatives and old friends. After decades in

America, I was once more able to recognize that I was also Serbian. Yugoslavia looked like both a business opportunity and, just possibly, a chance to help the country of my birth at a delicate time.

In 1990, I met John D. Scanlan, who had been the U.S. ambassador to Yugoslavia from 1985 to 1989, and we began what would be one of the most important and defining friendships of my life. A quintessential U.S. Foreign Service officer, Scanlan was self-effacing, distinguished, and above all pragmatic in a way that sharply contrasted with my style. With a unique ability to find his way to the root of a problem and the keenly honed sensibilities of a career diplomat, Scanlan understood better than most the importance of compromise and giving all sides in a dispute a way to save face. Scanlan had also studied Russian and Serbo-Croatian in college, and, although he had served in Russia, Poland, and South America beforehand, he was a passionate supporter of Yugoslavia and its people.

Scanlan's diplomatic career was nearing an end when we first met. We began to talk about Yugoslavia, but soon the conversation veered into personal matters, and I asked Scanlan about his future plans. He mentioned consulting, but he said that he still wasn't sure what he would do next. A week later, I called him: Would he want to come out to California and meet with me about a job? Scanlan was easily convinced to join ICN and oversee its Eastern European operations and expansion. He knew the language. He knew the powerbrokers. But neither of us realized then how close our relationship would become—and how much I would rely on Scanlan to navigate the minefield of Balkan politics in the near future.

In the early 1990s, we began to look carefully at Galenika, a large state-owned pharmaceutical company with offices and plant in a Belgrade suburb. Like most such state-owned firms in Eastern Europe, Galenika was lethargic, overstaffed, and badly in need of modernization. But it also had a decent product line, a solid position in its market, and the means to export to its neighbors. On the surface, this was an excellent business opportunity for what we believed would be an emerging Eastern European market. And I had ulterior motives. With ethnic tensions rising in the region once again, I believed that an economic revival could both spur growth and help to dampen rising nationalist urges.

In 1991, ICN acquired control of Galenika and became one of the first U.S. or European pharmaceutical companies to make a direct investment in Eastern Europe after the breakup of the USSR. The government retained a 25 percent interest. And, in what was then an imaginative and unusual approach to privatization, each of Galenika's 4,800 employees was given 203 shares of ICN stock, which would, by 2000, be worth over $3,600.

That done, Scanlan and I moved out into the rest of Eastern Europe, acquiring other state-owned companies. When we got to Russia, I found myself negotiating for the purchase of what would become five pharmaceutical plants in that country with Vladimir Putin, then a top aide to Anatoly Sobchak, the reformist mayor of St. Petersburg. I again proposed using ICN stock as a way of compensating workers. Putin liked the idea, but Russian workers are not allowed to own shares listed on the New York Stock Exchange. Instead, I deposited the shares in a bank and gave the workers certificates of ownership—exporting capitalism to the former Soviet Union one factory at a time. In any case, Putin would not be the last ruthless negotiator that I would have to contend with in the years to come.

3

A NATION COMES APART

As ICN's business relationship with Galenika flowered, I began making frequent trips to Belgrade, where I caught up with old friends, took an apartment in a luxury building, and even rented Tito's former office. But, for the time being, I stayed out of politics, even as the coalition of ethnic and religious groups that had been put together by Josip Tito at the end of World War II began to disintegrate in earnest.

In the 1940s, Tito had parlayed his leadership of the partisans into leadership of the Communist Party and the country. Abroad, he played East against West, or, more accurately, the Soviet Union against the United States. At home, he ruthlessly eliminated his enemies and competitors, abolished the Yugoslavian monarchy, and kept a firm grip on a Socialist federation of six republics with Tito-drawn borders—Slovenia, Bosnia/Herzegovina, Croatia, Montenegro, Macedonia—and Serbia, with two provinces that each had some political power of their own, Vojvodina in northern Serbia and Kosovo in the south.

Tito aspired to melt—some would have said hammer—the population together, but age-old ethnic differences continued to simmer despite the marshal's best efforts. At the end of his life, only slightly more than 5 percent of the people referred to themselves as "Yugoslavian," rather than identifying themselves as Serb, Slovenian, Albanian, or some other ethnic group (or in some cases Muslim, Serb Orthodox, or some other religious affiliation).

It was widely assumed by Westerners—and in the country itself, feared by some and hoped for by others—that the old tensions between ethnic and religious groups would rip Yugoslavia apart if Tito was no longer in charge. But the federation held together when he died in 1980, and the successful 1984 Winter Olympics in Sarajevo seemed to be a sign that the country could continue to survive as a coalition of peaceful neighbors. By the late 1980s, however, a series of disastrous economic mistakes led to inflation, unemployment, and stagnation. This downturn fed a growing distrust of each other by the republics, and particularly of Serbia. Serbians had long dominated the upper ranks of the country's bureaucracies and military services, and they appeared to get more than a just share of government support. Fueling dissension among the republics, nationalistic leaders often talked of "Greater Serbia"—that is, a pushing out of the republic's borders to encompass portions of its neighbors, particularly Bosnia and Croatia, which were heavily populated by Serbians.

In this regard, no Yugoslav leader was more inflammatory than Serbian president Slobodan Milosevic, who exploited simmering ethnic hatred for his own political gain. Milosevic was typical of the cold, humorless, and colorless apparatchik who rose through the ranks of the Communist parties across Eastern Europe and Russia, seemingly more through inertia than talent or force of personality. The writer Misha Glenny has concisely articulated the path to power that Milosevic took advantage of: "His success lies in the shameless exploitation of the most effective tools of Balkan politics: deception, corruption, blackmail, demagoguery and violence."

In 1987, Milosevic—then little known outside the country—had been sent to Kosovo to mediate a minor dispute between the province's Albanian majority and its Serbian minority. When Serbs complained of mistreatment by Albanian police, Milosevic uttered the words that would spark his political rise: "No one will ever dare beat you again." The effect on the crowd was electrifying. Milosevic's promise seemed to legitimize Serbian grievances, and it unleashed an outpouring of Serbian nationalist sentiment and anti-Albanian feeling. That event apparently confirmed for Milosevic that he could garner real political power by inciting latent Serbian nationalism.

Thus did Milosevic unleash on southeastern Europe the political genie that Tito had worked to keep in check for over four decades. With Serb populations spread throughout Yugoslavia, Tito had understood that direct appeals to Serbian pride and sentiment would only spread discord and mayhem—particularly in areas outside Serbia, such as Croatia and Bosnia, which had sizable Serb populations. Milosevic, on the other hand, began to organize frightening displays of Serb nationalism. This included busing in unemployed and disaffected Serb teenagers to ethnic tinderboxes such as Kosovo, a region of great historical importance to the largely Christian Serbs, yet one overwhelmingly populated by Albanian Muslims.

As many Serbian schoolboys could tell you, June 28 is the date of Serbia's 1389 defeat in the Battle of Kosovo. Outnumbered by a superior Ottoman Empire army, the Serb leader, Tsar Lazar, refused to surrender, and was defeated and himself killed—along with many of the Serbian elite and the head of the Ottoman forces. Although the battle itself was close to a draw, the Ottomans soon dominated much of what was Yugoslavia. The battle is now celebrated as a defeat that needs to be avenged, and Lazar remains a mythic hero to Serbs, as well as a saint in the Serbian Orthodox Church.

In 1989, in a celebration marking the six hundredth anniversary of the Kosovo battle, Milosevic established himself as a leader to be reckoned with in Yugoslavia. To provide the audience for his inflammatory speech, half a million Serbs had been brought from across the nation to Pristina, Kosovo's largest city and one heavily populated by Albanians. There, the political leaders from all of the country's republics, the cheering masses of Serbs, and a national television audience heard Milosevic proclaim that, after six centuries, Serbs were again confronting battle. His speech was frequently interrupted with chants comparing him to heroic Serbian leaders of the past. Within months, he was elected president of Serbia and the effective head of his party, with a dominant position in the Serbian state legislature and control of half of the federal votes—which he and his party had obtained by handpicking new leaders in Montenegro as well as Serbia, Kosovo, and Vojvodina.

Of all six Yugoslav republics, Slovenia had the smallest minority population. In a population of not quite two million people, over 1.7 million identified themselves as Slovene. The republic was also in better economic shape than the other members of the federation, contributed a disproportionate share of the federal budget, and generally seemed closer to its European neighbors—Austria, Hungary, and Italy—than to its fellow members of the federation. On June 25, 1991, Slovenia opted for independence.

Milosevic and the Serb-dominated JNA, the Yugoslav National Army, first thought that a simple show of force would keep the republic from seceding. But Slovenia had been preparing for the possibility of conflict. It quickly mobilized 21,000 men, threw back lightly armed Yugoslav units, and ran a masterful public relations campaign. When a federal government airstrike killed several foreign truckers, most of the already sympathetic Western press praised Slovenia and condemned the Yugoslavians. At a cost of less than sixty lives, the war was over in days. Belgrade accepted Slovenia's independence on July 18.

However, Milosevic was not about to give up quickly or easily when it came to Croatia, which declared its own independence just one day after the Slovenia announcement. Over a half million Serbs lived in eastern Croatia. Wounds from the Ustase's actions during World War II had never healed for many of them, as well as for many in Serbia proper. Here was the opportunity both to settle old scores and to make clear who were the true masters of Yugoslavia. Civilians were massacred as the ancient cities of Dubrovnik and Vukovar were bombed into submission. Eventually, the fighting came to an end with some twenty thousand dead and Croatia divided into ethnic enclaves, foreshadowing the catastrophe about to erupt in Bosnia-Herzegovina.

In March 1991, the European Parliament passed a resolution that the Yugoslav republics and autonomous regions must have the right to determine their own future, "in a peaceful and democratic manner, and on the basis of recognized international and internal borders." But the Western European governments were not united. With secessionist movements of their own to worry about, Britain, France, and Spain especially were concerned about setting a precedent they themselves would not be keen to follow, and they feared the consequences of any involvement by other nations in Yugoslavian affairs.

In December 1991, however, Germany's foreign minister, Hans Dietrich Genscher, said that if the then European Commission failed to recognize Croatia, Germany would act unilaterally. As Germany was the strongest power on the continent, the rest of Europe had little choice but to take into account and abide by German intentions. Cyrus Vance, the former American secretary of state who had been appointed UN peace negotiator, and Lord Carrington, the former British foreign secretary who was the European Union peace envoy, argued that withholding recognition was the only weapon available to achieve a peaceful settlement. But on December 23, 1991, true to their word, Germany recognized Slovenia and Croatia.

The recognition of Croatia unleashed a chain reaction of diplomatic maneuvers. Once Croatia achieved independence, Bosnia was unlikely to remain part of a Serbian-dominated Yugoslavia. Home to three ethnic groups—Serbs, Croats, and Muslims—it had the potential to plunge the Balkans into cataclysmic violence. Many in the West who supported Croatia's and Slovenia's secession nevertheless urged restraint with Bosnia.

Bosnia's president, Alija Izetbegovic, argued that if Croatia was recognized as an independent state, why should recognition be withheld from Bosnia? Yet, he fatally underestimated the opposition he would encounter from Belgrade and the Serbs within Bosnia. Within hours of the Bosnian declaration of independence in April 1992, violence erupted. Supporters of Bosnian Serb leader Radovan Karadzic, who declared the new state stillborn, opened up their guns on Muslim demonstrators in Sarajevo, killing a number of protesters. Then nearly the whole of Bosnia exploded in an orgy of genocidal brutality, and the deadly passions long suppressed by Tito and inflamed by Milosevic erupted across the Balkans. War was on.

4

A DAMN FOOL IDEA

Slobodan Milosevic knew he needed friends, or at least connections, in the West—particularly in the United States. But his relationship with any Americans with whom he had been friendly in earlier years had cooled. He needed new help and shortly began to think that recently returned American businessman and Serbia's prodigal son Milan Panic might be the one to supply it. Milosevic was impressed, I think, by my wealth and political connections. His experience had taught him that access often equals influence, and, with my connections in the Democratic Party, I certainly appeared to have access to the top layers of U.S. political power.

In early March 1992, with conflict under way in Bosnia, I had flown to Belgrade for an ICN management meeting. I was sitting in my fifteenth-floor office when an aide came in with a message: I was invited to join President Milosevic for dinner that evening. Though I had met Milosevic on a number of occasions, this would be our first one-on-one encounter.

That night, I arrived at the Serbian presidential building, an often-gloomy, late-nineteenth-century edifice in the old center of Belgrade. Milosevic's first-floor office was a suite of three interconnected rooms: a waiting room to the right, his personal secretary's room in the middle, and his own office to the left, leading off to a series of rooms he used for official dinners. Dinner was served in the office. We talked for a while about the reconstruction of Yugoslavia's economy. But after two bottles of wine, the conversation grew more intimate. The slightly inebriated president said, "You know, Milan, you could be a good prime minister of Yugoslavia." I laughed off the comment. "Of course I would," I joked. In truth I had long believed that, if put in charge, I could help to reform Serbia's economy for the better.

"I'm not joking," Milosevic insisted. "Why don't you come over and run our economy? I'll do the rest. Think about it. We need you, Milan," Milosevic told me. Of course, what Milosevic really wanted, it is now clear, was a figurehead. In his biography of Milosevic, British journalist Adam Lebor writes that it was Dusan Mitevic, a Milosevic aide and the director of Belgrade Television, who first broached the idea of my appointment. "I thought," he reports Mitevic saying, "we should work peacefully with the opposition parties. That's why I brought in Panic. My idea was that instead of presenting ourselves as a Communist country, we would have a rich American imperialist as prime minister."

Still, I went home with my head swimming as much from the Milosevic proposal as the wine. The idea was crazy, not the least because Milosevic was not a man I would normally involve myself with. But here was an opportunity to make a real difference. I could help end the war and put my homeland on the path to economic revival. In any case, the Balkans were in such a hell that somebody needed to go there to help. They were going to start to kill each other, and I thought I could stop it. I called Scanlan and told him about the dinner. Scanlan thought the drunken episode was nothing more than Balkan hot air. "Milan, I don't think you want to get involved in the politics of this country," he warned me. "It's a mess and it's only going to get worse."

I made no mention of the offer when Scanlan and I flew to Budapest the next day. "I thought I'd heard the last of it," Scanlan said later. But, once the seed had been planted, I wouldn't give up the idea that easily. I had considered running for political office in California, but had ruled it out. I knew my own personality well enough to understand that I could never absorb the personal abuse of an American political campaign. I had been shaken by the ferocity of attacks on Michael Dukakis, Jimmy Carter, and other Democrats I had supported. An election campaign, I concluded, was interesting so long as I was only an observer. Here, however, was a different route to power. I wouldn't have to wade into the swampy morass of politics. I could simply be appointed to the position, and then could focus my energy on making a meaningful contribution to the future of my native land. Unlike many politicians, in

Serbia and elsewhere, who went into politics to gain wealth and privilege, I was interested in neither. After all, I already had all that.

Before leaving for Budapest, I quietly contacted Dusan Mitevic and asked him to tell the dictator that I was willing to consider the offer. Then, for the next few weeks, I thought of little else. Everything about Milosevic's offer excited me. It opened up a range of wholly unexpected opportunities, but most of all it gave me a chance to leave a lasting legacy on my native land, and to help it move in the direction of political and economic freedom that I myself had embraced. What CEO has not fantasized about running an entire country? For a businessman, the greatest glory is to take over a bad company and turn it around. And with Yugoslavia at that dark time, I had a bad one.

I also believed I could entice multinational corporations to invest in the country. I planned to hire the best brains from American universities and think tanks and bring them to Belgrade to help reorganize the national economy. And I would work with the legislature to create an investment and financial environment conducive to economic growth: low inflation, stable rules of the game for business, and a climate friendly to foreign investors. On top of it all, almost overnight I would become a major actor in one of the most pressing international crises of the time—a crisis that demanded resolution and enlightened leadership, and one whose contours I had known since childhood. How could I turn down that possibility?

So I quietly campaigned for the job—but I at first kept my intentions secret even from those close to me, including my second wife, Sally Panic. Sally recalls that I first suggested the idea as a joke, and had laughed after saying, "They may want me to come over and run their country." "I laughed, too," Sally remembered. "I had no idea he was serious. He never said he was about to make a major decision. That's just the way he is."

In time, however, I began dropping hints to close associates. I asked Birch Bayh if one could retain American citizenship while serving as prime minister of another country. Bayh had lost his Indiana Senate seat in the 1980 election but stayed in Washington as a law firm partner. It didn't take long for him to figure out what I was up to. "I was very negative about it," Bayh said later. "I thought it was another of Milan's unpredictable escapades that would never come to fruition. The man is larger than life, but what a damn fool idea." These concerns notwith-

standing, Bayh told me that it indeed was possible, citing the example of
Meir Kahane, a Jewish activist in New York who had been elected to
the Israeli Knesset. When stripped of his American citizenship, Kahane
had challenged the decision in court and won.

When I returned to Belgrade for a short trip later in March 1992, I
brought Scanlan along for a meeting with Milosevic in the dark and
empty presidential palace. Scanlan recalls wincing when I suggested
that we offer good advice to the dictator. "We can help them a bit with
the public relations, Jack. We can put them in touch with the right
people in Washington." In fact, I had already done some work in this
regard. I previously had entered a joint venture with Belgrade Television to help pay for cable distribution of Belgrade TV News in the
United States. And I had sponsored a celebration in 1990 commemorat-
ing nine decades of diplomatic relations between Serbia and the United
States.

Nevertheless, at the meeting Scanlan remembers telling Milosevic:
"Slobo, your public relations stink. I don't want to speak about the
merits of the case. I will disagree with you. But the fact is that you're
not making your case well. The Slovenes and Croatians are doing a
masterful job." Surprisingly, Milosevic agreed with Scanlan. "Our PR *is*
bad. What do you think we ought to do?" "Don't you understand?"
Scanlan replied. "One of the themes the Croatians have succeeded in
peddling in the West is that they are democrats and you are still a
communist!" Scanlan said. "Build a big bonfire in the center of Belgrade and throw into it every goddamn red star you can find," the
former ambassador counseled. "It takes that kind of action to show the
world you're not a Bolshevik."

But that was something that Milosevic could not do. His appeals to
Serbian nationalism aside, the old Communist establishment was his
only solid political base. He had come to power riding the waves of a
movement fused by socialism and nationalism. But a series of setbacks
on all fronts had led to widespread discontent and despair among the
populace. They had lost faith in Milosevic, and by early 1992, much of
the population had turned against him. Truth be told, Milosevic wasn't
looking for a public relations solution. He simply wanted to maintain his
grip on power—a grip that he was slowly losing.

There was a growing feeling among the professional class in Belgrade that only an outside agent, someone untainted by the Communist

past, could help Serbia repair its image. Even the nationalist intellectuals who had played a crucial role in Milosevic's rise to power began to think that Serbia was heading toward catastrophe. The most prominent among them, the novelist Dobrica Cosic and the poet Matija Backovic, began distancing themselves from Milosevic and the regime. Cosic, regarded by many as the "Father of the Nation," withdrew from public life. His allies, ostensibly still in Milosevic's corner, began secretly plotting, convinced that Milosevic must be removed from power.

For his part, Cosic had long supported the idea of Greater Serbia. In 1986, he had helped write an influential memorandum to the Serbian Academy of Arts and Sciences that accused Tito of undermining Serbian power and influence—Milosevic had used this document to pave his own rise to power. However, while Cosic was a nationalist, he was also a realist. The recognition of Bosnian independence by the United States and other Western nations, as well as the increasingly brutal episodes of ethnic cleansing in Bosnia, helped to convince him that the dream was dead. He and his allies just wanted to salvage what they could—which at this point meant removing Milosevic.

The conspirators cast a wide net throughout the political, military, and security establishment. They also tried to win the support of the West. The American ambassador, Warren Zimmermann, recalled in his memoirs how Bosnian Serb vice president Nikola Koljevic came to his residence one Saturday morning in May. "After some aimless conversation, he came to the point," Zimmermann wrote. "He had been talking to Dobrica Cosic. The two of them agreed that Milosevic had become a liability for Serbia. It was time to replace him. Koljevic told me that Cosic would be much better as president of Serbia." The removal of Milosevic, Koljevic added, would eliminate a major international problem.

Zimmermann said he gave Koljevic no encouragement, in part because Koljevic had been closely identified with Milosevic's policies and Zimmermann feared a provocation. In any case, the incident was quickly forgotten, as Washington ordered the ambassador to return home in protest over the Bosnian war. Even so, Milosevic was boxed in on the left and right. Facing both growing domestic opposition to his rule and the emerging impact of international sanctions, the Serbian president was now barely hanging onto power. The other shoe seemed to drop in

May and June, as huge crowds of Serbs gathered in the streets of Belgrade to protest his rule and demand he step down.

With the opposition being joined by some of the most respected citizens in the land, Milosevic feared that if he used force against the protestors, he would incite open rebellion. But ever the cagey tactician, Milosevic still had a few cards to play. He first placated the nationalists by offering Cosic the now largely ceremonial post of president of Yugoslavia. Next Milosevic needed to bring me into the fold. He believed that my presence would both quiet the liberal opposition and curry favor with the United States. Most of all, Milosevic thought, I could use my influence with Western policy makers to have sanctions lifted against the country. Milosevic calculated that I could be seduced by the pomp and ceremony of the new position, all the while leaving real power in his hands.

Back in California, I contacted Ambassador Zimmermann, who was visiting Los Angeles to address the World Affairs Council. "He told me about Milosevic's offer," recalled Zimmermann. "Obviously I could not give him any advice, but I could tell him one thing; 'Milosevic is not somebody who was going to share power with anybody. That's just the way Milosevic is.'" To this line of advice, I replied: "He doesn't know Milan Panic."

I also contacted my friend Bill Press, a television commentator in Los Angeles and former top aide to California governor Jerry Brown, and sought his help dealing with the Bush administration. Sanctions against what remained of Yugoslavia made it impossible for Americans to do business with Serbia, let alone serve in its government. At first, Press tried to dissuade me from even considering Milosevic's offer. But, sensing that I had already determined to fight for what I wanted, Press took me to meet with Republican strategist Roger Ailes, who obtained word from the White House that they would not necessarily stand in my way. But, of course, as soon became evident, that didn't mean they would help me, either.

The official announcement was made in time-honored Balkan fashion. First came rumors that Cosic and I would enter Yugoslav politics—rumors nobody in a position of authority would confirm. This was soon followed by informed speculation in official circles. For those who could put two and two together, it all added up. By the time the official news agency announced on June 14 that I had been offered the job of prime minister, few political observers were surprised. Nonetheless, the announcement was greeted by an extraordinary popular response in Serbia, and especially in Belgrade.

I got the news while I was sailing aboard my yacht off the California coast with my wife, Sally; my stepson, Mark Taylor; and an old friend and ICN vice president, Ted Olic. Telegrams and messages of support piled up in the ICN offices. But, fearing for my safety, Sally tried to dissuade me. Olic also told me it was a mistake to accept. And no one was more dismissive than Jack Scanlan, who told me, "You can't accept an offer coming from Milosevic and his political allies. You will look like Milosevic's puppet." Scanlan also reminded me that Milosevic topped the list of most disliked personalities in the world. "But I want it, Jack," I responded to my friend. "You've got to help me. Milosevic thinks he can corrupt me, but I'm telling you he's wrong."

Scanlan understood that I would need more than self-confidence to succeed against the odds. I needed political legitimacy, the support of Serbian political leaders. In Scanlan's view, I had to demand that the offer would only be accepted if it was endorsed by all political parties, including the opposition. Birch Bayh agreed with this approach. I should set conditions: first, that the invitation had to be endorsed by all political parties, and second, that the acceptance was conditional on me retaining my U.S. citizenship.

With the decision made, the machinery was set in motion. After a seemingly endless series of debates in my inner circle, a statement was drafted by Scanlan and issued to the Yugoslav news agency. I said I was deeply honored by the offer, but I made clear that the future prime minister of Yugoslavia must have the full support not only of the ruling parties, but also of all other parties, including prominent members of the Academy of Sciences and business leaders, as a precondition for success. Since this was not currently the case, I said, I was not in the position to accept the offer made public in Belgrade today.

This maneuver left Milosevic baffled. Having in effect already announced my selection as prime minister, his maneuvering space had shrunk dramatically. Luckily, and uncharacteristically, the opposition was more than happy to lend a hand. They promptly endorsed me. Patriarch Pavle, the leader of the Serbian church, fired off a telegram urging me to take the job. The Serbian Academy of Sciences came next, issuing a statement endorsing my candidacy.

And so, with the preconditions met, I gladly took up the offer, even though I would do so officially only a day before departing for Belgrade. In the meantime, Scanlan urged me to fly to Washington as soon as possible. Nailing down official support from the United States would be essential, he thought, if I had any hope of success.

By June, however, the war in Bosnia was more than just a foreign policy problem for the Bush administration. It had become a domestic political issue, as reports of ethnic cleansing and pictures of emaciated Muslim prisoners horrified the American people. Public pressure on the administration was growing, and George H. W. Bush, engaged in a tough reelection campaign despite enjoying overwhelming public support during the Iraq War the year before, watched with alarm as his popularity dropped steadily. President Bush had no interest in being dragged into another war right before an election. Moreover, his aides would later report, the situation was one that only seemed to confuse the president, who appeared unsure about what was going on in the complicated, contentious Balkans.

In a last-ditch attempt to stop the breakup of Yugoslavia, Bush's secretary of state, James Baker, had visited the region in June 1991. In a one-day visit, he met with Yugoslav president Ante Markovic as well as all six leaders of the country's republics. But he found himself frustrated by the meetings. Secretary Baker was unsparing in his criticism of Milosevic, who, he believed, was the instigator of Yugoslavia's breakup. But Milosevic apparently concluded, correctly at the time, that the Americans would limit their efforts to diplomacy and not use military force. Upon Baker's return, he had concluded, "We got no dog in that fight." The administration's aim was to let the Europeans take the lead. Why should the United States put its credibility and diplomatic capital on the line for a country lacking in geopolitical significance?

Once it was clear that the world's greatest superpower had only limited interest in the Balkan situation, however, Yugoslavia's regional leaders began to believe they had virtual carte blanche to do as they pleased. I have always believed that Baker's visit in 1991 was a major failure of U.S. diplomacy. Not surprisingly, the Bush administration was not pleased by my plans. In their view, by accepting Milosevic's offer, I was forcing the administration to become involved in the Balkans, something it clearly did not want to do.

Overnight, the "green light" I had received from Roger Ailes turned red. A series of bureaucratic hurdles were erected to thwart my effort. The State Department declared that an American citizen could not hold public office in another country. If I left for Yugoslavia, I would lose my U.S. citizenship. That would have been a bridge too far for me—I did not want to give up my stake in my adopted home. Instead, feeling increasingly impatient, I sprang into action. A retinue of aides and advisors came cross-country with me to Washington's Willard Hotel. We took two large rooms in the hotel basement, set up batteries of telephones and faxes, and began a propaganda war of our own.

The key figures in this effort were David Calef, an ICN manager with a resume full of political experience going back to his days as a student activist at Berkeley in the 1960s, and Bill Press, who knew many Democratic and Republican members of California's congressional delegation. The two Californians put in overtime, working the phones and reaching out to every contact they had in the government. They generated a flood of letters into the White House from scores of senators, congressmen, prominent personalities, and business leaders, mostly Democrats but also centrist Republicans such as Senator Richard Lugar. A fellow Serb, Republican governor George Voinovich of Ohio, weighed in as well, writing to the president: "At this point, Mr. President, Mr. Panic needs your support. I beg you to review [his] plans, give your approval and support and open up discussions with [him]."

Despite the intense lobbying blitz, the administration continued to stonewall. For a Democrat without any substantive political bridge into a Republican White House, my last hope was Lawrence Eagleburger, deputy secretary of state and Scanlan's old friend and patron. Eagleburger was a brilliant, blunt, chain-smoking workaholic whose informal and unpretentious style had gained him respect both at home and abroad. Eight years as Kissinger's top aide during the Nixon and Ford administrations had turned him into a true Washington insider. But he was at the same time an experienced and well-liked American diplomat, soon to reach the height of his career as secretary of state.

The situation in the Balkans was, I think, agonizing for Eagleburger. As a young Foreign Service officer, he had begun his career there in 1962, spending eight years in the region. Later in the 1970s, he served as U.S. ambassador to Yugoslavia with Scanlan as his deputy. Eagleburger wanted to do something to help a nation he loved. But at the same time, he felt particularly vulnerable to criticism because of his former links to Milosevic and other Serbs: When Eagleburger served as ambassador to Belgrade, Milosevic was a young Communist banker who was a frequent guest at Eagleburger's table and, playing his role to a tee, often talked the liberal economics Americans wanted to hear. Eagleburger also understood the complexities of Yugoslavia as well as anyone in the State Department, and this understanding appeared to have made him grim and fatalistic about prospects in the Balkans. He seemed to believe that nothing of positive import could be accomplished by outsiders, and that each Yugoslavian faction would not be satisfied until it had killed off all or most of the others.

Eagleburger also understood how the president and his advisors felt: The Bush administration was caught in the middle of an election campaign that left little room for foreign entanglements. President Bush was already being hammered for his inattention to domestic affairs, including a serious economic recession, at the expense of foreign policy. High-level involvement in the Balkans was the last thing he needed. And finally, as he once put it dryly, "I look with great disfavor on an American citizen who wants to run another country. It is a prejudice on my part." An Eagleburger aide later recalled that "Larry never once gave Panic a chance. He was convinced that he was a puppet of Milosevic, and he kept referring to him as 'that fool' or 'that goddamn idiot.'" Another official put it this way: "We all thought Panic was a lightweight. Maybe we were wrong, but that was the way we viewed him. The fact is, he was a mystery to us and we had no control over him."

A veteran hand at State himself, Scanlan was staggered, but not altogether surprised, by the "consummate ill will" toward me from the very outset. Almost immediately, there was corridor gossip in Foggy Bottom that I was a flake, a clown, a Serb apologist, a combination of rich buffoon and political neophyte. Washington's foreign policy priesthood regarded me with an eye-rolling disdain. From their perspective, the world was their responsibility, and eyebrows arched whenever I appeared on television and talked with assurance about my plan to bring peace to the former Yugoslavia.

If anything, the behind-the-scenes attacks on poor Scanlan were even more scathing. I was considered just a bumbling tourist, but Scanlan was once a Washington insider himself who had been anointed and served his time in the diplomatic priesthood. Now he was considered a heretic, an apostate, a sellout. Over the years, many senior diplomats, including Henry Kissinger, had profited by advising foreign governments. But rude stories about Scanlan began to circulate. "Prostitution," some of his colleagues called it. He had become my "hired gun."

Had Scanlan been told directly to abandon the entire enterprise, I think he probably would have. Turning his back on the State Department was, for him, one of the hardest things he ever had to do. But he also came to believe that I could succeed where so many others had failed. The fact that he could not get his old colleagues to see the potential in my administration only produced more stress for him. Scanlan thought I at least had a puncher's chance, and maybe even an excellent chance, to make a positive difference in the Balkans—but only if the United States threw its backing behind me.

As a former State Department official, Scanlan thought that the policy positions he and I developed were in line with U.S. objectives, except that they emphasized a political rather than military solution. But many top State officials thought of these political solutions as more discussion at the expense of action, and the type of weak-kneed, vacillating approach preferred by the United Nations and the Western allies.

Even beyond that, Scanlan's biggest impediment was that he was seen to be on the wrong side of the conflict. "The feeling in the department was that the Serbs were really the worst actors in this drama. Therefore Jack was quickly discredited as an apologist for the Serbs," one senior diplomat said. For Birch Bayh, the quintessential Washington insider, it was clear from early on that neither Scanlan nor I would be able to get the United States to see the Balkan conflict with a more balanced view. "They invariably turned any statement of fact into a question of motive," said Bayh. "It was as though Panic were radioactive, which had something to do with the public relations war as reflected on the pages of the *New York Times* and the *Washington Post*. There was a general feeling, from what you read in the two papers, that the Serbs were the Nazis of the region. The Croats and Muslims had done a fantastic job in public relations. If everything the American people learned about the Serbs came from CNN, how could one blame them for assuming that they were people without a soul?"

These anti-Serb attitudes undoubtedly contributed to the extended delay in receiving the American government's permission to accept the prime minister position in Belgrade. I became so frustrated that at one point I considered going over without a license, which would have resulted in criminal charges and the freezing of my assets. Ultimately, my inner circle objected. "Scanlan and I vowed we'd throw ourselves in front of the airplane if he tried to leave before this was resolved," Bayh said. In the end, Bayh's involvement was critical. He presented the State Department with a detailed analysis of the Supreme Court decision in the Meir Kahane case. Why should I be treated any differently?

"What about Panic taking an oath of office to a foreign country?" argued one State Department legal expert. Bayh countered that he and Scanlan would craft the oath so that its wording did not violate the U.S. Constitution. I was forced to resign my ICN chairmanship and give up control of my company, which was handed over to trusted executives Adam Jerney and Roberts Smith. But even after all that, other technical delays arose. By the beginning of July, I had lost patience. On July 2, I issued a statement to the Yugoslav media announcing that I had accepted the offer to become prime minister. In the face of such determination, the administration yielded. "We got the license after he was already in the air," Bayh said later. "I only let him go because I was reasonably sure he'd get it."

Thirty thousand feet over the Atlantic, I took a moment for self-reflection, and, perhaps uncharacteristically for me, grappled with some of the doubts that accompany buyer's remorse. I secretly fretted about my patchy education. I was not an intellectual. I was not a politician. Could I really pull this off? But my natural optimism pushed these thoughts aside. As the contours of my native land came into view, I could not help but think of my dear mother, Zora, who had died five years earlier. My only regret then was that she had not lived to see me become Yugoslavia's prime minister. She would have been so very proud.

5

MR. PRIME MINISTER

Within mere moments of my arrival in Belgrade, Slobodan Milosevic had cause to believe that he had seriously misjudged me. To accompany me back to Belgrade from the Budapest airport (because of sanctions against Yugoslavia, international flights could not land in Belgrade), Milosevic had dispatched his loyal aide Dusan Mitevic. But Mitevic by then was thoroughly despised by the Serbian people—in some cases more than Milosevic. Student demonstrations had even been organized to attack him. When Scanlan saw Mitevic at the Budapest airport, he quickly realized how bad it would be for me to be seen with an individual so closely tied to the regime at the onset of my tenure. It was essential, Scanlan thought, that the Serbian people view their new prime minister as a fresh and independent face.

In no uncertain terms, Scanlan told me that I must not allow Mitevic to accompany us. "You will be dead on arrival," he said. I wavered—I actually felt bad for Mitevic. But after much cajoling from Scanlan, I relented and refused to let Mitevic join us for the trip across the border and to Belgrade. For Jack, this was a worrying sign. He told me I would have to be a lot tougher than this brief airport interlude if I was going to take on a dictator like Slobodan Milosevic.

Left alone at the airport in Budapest, Mitevic was forced to rent a car and drive himself back to Serbia. I later heard that, after crossing the frontier into Yugoslavia late that evening, he rushed into the border police office to call Milosevic at home. He described what happened, and the cold shoulder he received from me and my people. "I thought I was looking at a conspiratorial group," he added. Milosevic kept silent for a while, then groaned, *"Jebo te bog, sta cemo sada?"* The English translation of this is rather straightforward: "Holy shit, what are we going to do now?"

Once again, the dictator found himself with grave concerns about his political future. This was a man who came from a family of deep depressives. Several committed suicide. His father, a defrocked priest, shot himself in the head. His mother hanged herself from a living room light-fixture. His favorite uncle, a Communist war hero, also took his own life. Compounding matters, Milosevic was used to dealing exclusively with sycophants and yes-men. He looked to others to take on the hard work that he was unable and unwilling to do himself. Behind the scenes he was deeply involved in fomenting hatred and prosecuting war, but Milosevic always sought to present to his people and to the world an image of noninvolvement. This was a politician who left no tracks—one who never sat for interviews or wrote articles under his own name. His speeches contained no plans, just primitive slogans designed for a nationalist ear. In sum, Milosevic was not just a dangerously unstable leader, but a well-practiced and exquisite liar.

I was supposed to have been Milosevic's public relations general, a smiling, reasonable face that could be trotted out and presented to the world. He thought he had me figured out: A little flattery and obsequiousness would ensure my compliance. But, as Milosevic would soon find out, I had other plans. With sanctions beginning to take a toll on the Serbian people, and with a new prime minister who clearly had his own agenda, Milosevic, I believe, quickly realized that his choices were, yet again, narrowing.

That was certainly my view as well. Even before I boarded the plane to Yugoslavia, I knew that Milosevic must leave office for Serbia to have any kind of future. Only then would there be an end to the sanctions, and the process of economic reconstruction could begin. I wanted to turn Serbia into the California of Europe, overhauling the archaic political and economic edifices of Communism and introducing American political, economic, and social values. But, this could only be realistically achieved if Milosevic was no longer on the scene. Scanlan had pleaded with me to only go to Serbia *after* Milosevic had stepped down, but at the time I was unconcerned. I was confident in my persuasive powers.

On my first night in Belgrade, it seemed I had reason to be. After a grueling seventeen-hour trip via Budapest, I was greeted by cheering throngs as I walked down Prince Michael Street in the city center. "Save us, Milan!" the crowds yelled. "You are our hope!" For more than a week, antigovernment protests in the city had been swelling, and my presence only added to their fervor. Ever the American patriot, I quoted John F. Kennedy's famous dictum: "Ask not what your country can do for you, ask what you can do for your country." At my first press conference, I summed up my approach to governing: "It is better to negotiate and even quarrel for years than to wage war for even one day." When asked my priorities, I said, "Stop the war, stop the killing, stop the war."

The Serbian people immediately took to me. I am not a strong public speaker, though I believe I can be eloquent and convincing in small, private meetings. But no one even seemed to mind that I spoke Serbo-Croatian with a heavy accent. If anything, my thick accent and poor grammar seemed to endear me to ordinary Serbs. I think the people recognized that, for all my businessman's brashness, I am a truthful man who was seeking to help. In Serbia, my substantial personal wealth had been exaggerated to equal that of Bill Gates or the Rockefellers. But instead of making me seem unapproachable, I think it helped bring a sense of authenticity to what I was seeking to do. Four decades of Communism had merely reaffirmed the traditional attitude of the Serbian people toward authority: Public life was nothing more than a means for accumulating privileges and wealth. Yet here was a man who sought power, not for personal gain, but for the common good.

To the man and woman on the street, I was both an exotic visitor from a distant land and, at the same time, "*nash*"—one of ours. For those who did not live in Serbia at the time, it's almost impossible to understand the Serbian people's desperate desire for change in the summer of 1992, and the hope they invested in me. The economy was a shambles and living standards had fallen dramatically. In 1990, the average income per person stood at 800 deutschmarks per month—by 1992 that figure had been reduced to about 100 deutschemarks. Whole swaths of Serbian society were on the verge of poverty. Above all, Serbs were deeply uncomfortable with their newly acquired notoriety. They had fought bravely against the Germans and Austrians in World War I and against the Nazis in World War II. To go from a valiant people to international pariah was more than some could bear.

I knew the task ahead of me, and I wasted little time in seeking to establish my legitimacy. I made clear that my first order of business would be to ease Milosevic out of office and clear the way for the lifting of UN economic sanctions. After being in the country for only a few days, I met with Milosevic to apprise him of the plan. Cutting through the usual niceties, I shook the Serbian strongman's hand and asked, "Well, Slobo, when are you stepping down?" Milosevic seemed momentarily taken back, but I continued. "The moment I take over the prime minister's job," I told him, "your role as Serbia's leader is over. Do you understand that?" Milosevic answered, "I understand." Just to make sure there was no confusion, I delivered an ultimatum: "Now I'll give you five minutes to think it over and decide. You tell me whether I should stay here or go back. If you want me to stay, I will say that you are ill and that you need a rest." Milosevic looked glum. "Fine, you're staying," he said after a long pause.

To move the process forward, I offered Milosevic a golden parachute, in the form of the presidency of a new American-Yugoslav bank I was in the process of creating. Milosevic would move to California, where, in addition to a $150,000 annual salary, he would be given a mansion, a yacht, and a variety of other perks. I even offered to let Milosevic stay on my boat for a few months if it would get him to step down.

As the reality of his departure finally hit him, Milosevic looked ashen and abandoned. I felt sorry for him—his emotional distress was visible. I even tried to console him: "History will remember your personal sacrifice for the Serbian people," I told Milosevic. "You are going to become a new hero in the people's eyes, because you are resigning so that the sanctions can be lifted."

Milosevic continued to insist that he would only leave office if I could persuade the UN to lift international sanctions. That was my next chore. We shook hands and shared a—celebratory for me, funereal for Milosevic—drink. Knowing the Serbian president's reputation as a skilled operator all too well, I insisted that the agreement be put in writing. Mitevic and Jack were assigned the job. They spent two days arguing over every phrase before the document was presented to the principals. In the end, however, Milosevic never signed the document. He later told Mitevic to simply forget the whole thing.

Dusan Mitevic believed that Slobodan may have initially felt he had little choice. "I think Milosevic felt cornered," he recalls. "Before the UN sanctions were imposed, we didn't quite grasp what that would mean for the country. But a month later we were suffocating, there was no oxygen. Milosevic may have looked at Panic's proposal as a way out." Most observers, including Jack Scanlan, thought that Milosevic never intended to give up power in this fashion, but there is no doubt that he must have been fully aware of his vulnerability. It is also likely that his wife, Mira, could not fathom the thought of giving in, and steeled his nerve.

In any event, convinced at the time that Milosevic's voluntary departure was a done deal, I promptly went about setting the wheels in motion for the next item of business—getting the UN sanctions removed. As it happened, just then secretary of state James Baker sent a telegram to me urging a meeting in Helsinki, where Baker would soon attend the Conference on Security and Cooperation in Europe (an organization that had just suspended Yugoslavia's membership). Brimming with optimism, I rushed to Helsinki on July 8. It would be my arrival on the international diplomatic stage, and one that I would never forget.

The meeting took place in the "bubble," or secure area of the U.S. Embassy in Helsinki, with Scanlan and Ambassador Thomas Niles also on hand. It did not go well. Trained as a businessman, I now confess I was unprepared for the world of diplomacy. I had always prided myself on being able to sit down with any man, talk things out, and find some common ground. But James Baker was a different creature altogether. I later joked that Jack had three heart attacks during the meeting.

"Here's what we expect you to do," Baker began as he read from a single sheet of paper. He called on Yugoslavia to remove heavy weapons from Bosnia, support the UN relief supplies effort, and recognize the country's independence. "We expect deeds, not words," he plainly stated. I interrupted him to open the negotiations in the way a businessman would. "I agree with your assessments, now let's talk." But Baker would not relent. "Mr. Panic, you've got to stop interrupting me, I've got to get through these points." "Why don't you just give me your paper and we talk?" I asked. "No, no"—Baker bristled—"I'll read it and then we can talk."

Exasperated, I tried to regain my composure. I candidly confessed to Baker that this whole experience made me nervous and I was probably a bit overenthusiastic. Then I sat back and listened: The United States wanted my government to end all financial and military support for Karadzic, the Bosnian Serb leader; stop supplying Serb irregulars in Bosnia; and begin a dialogue with the Albanians in Kosovo. I willingly agreed to all the points and then tried to steer the conversation to what I believed was the crux of the matter in the Balkans—Slobodan Milosevic. I told Baker that Milosevic had agreed to resign, on condition that the UN lift sanctions against Yugoslavia, and asked that the United States do its part to help remove them—in particular the ban on oil imports. I fully expected the U.S. secretary of state to be thrilled by the news and eager to lend a hand. But Baker wasn't interested. On the issue of sanctions, he said, "That is a question for the United Nations." As for getting rid of Milosevic, "How do we know he wouldn't be replaced by somebody worse?" Baker asked.

I was stunned. Here I was giving the West a golden opportunity to remove the one man more responsible than any other for the ongoing instability in the Balkans, and the U.S. secretary of state was unmoved, even dismissive. "There's nobody else," I told him. "I'm prime minister. All you have to do is give something to the Serbian people." Once Milosevic was removed from power, I insisted, things would be different. The conversation continued in the same spirit for a while, as Baker refused to give any ground and I continued to push him toward a stronger signal of support for my new administration.

Before parting, Baker told me how much he admired my courage in taking on a difficult responsibility. But later, he told the *Washington Post*, "I can't judge for you how effective he'll be. . . . They may roll over him. He's been a pretty successful and effective businessman, and yet I don't think he's done a lot of political work that I'm aware of." "Baker did a number on Milan," Jack said later. Both he and I began to believe it might not be possible to get Washington on our side.

My diplomatic foray in Helsinki was not yet finished. On the same day of my ill-fated meeting with Baker, I sought to break the impasse in Serb-Croat relations during a meeting with Croatian leaders. The dispute between the two groups troubled and mystified me, and I spoke bluntly with Croatian president Franjo Tudjman. I told Tudjman that now that the republics of the former Yugoslavia had gained their independence, it was time for both sides to accept facts on the ground and move forward with a rapprochement.

"The current situation is not satisfactory," Tudjman agreed. The Belgrade-Zagreb highway had been closed, so I suggested reopening the connection between the two capitals as a symbol of easing relations. I believed the agreement would symbolize the beginning of a cooperative relationship between Serbs and Croats. Moreover, I knew if I was to succeed I would have to work closely with a man like Tudjman. I believed a carrot offered today could lead to better relations and possibly reconciliation down the road.

A grim Tudjman had other ideas. He interrupted me, reminding me that Belgrade still refused to recognize Croatian sovereignty. "Let me make myself perfectly clear," Tudjman sternly told me. "First you have to recognize Croatia, and then we can move to other things." Fine," I responded. "We'll recognize Croatia!" "You are willing to recognize Croatia within Tito's borders?" Tudjman asked incredulously. "Yes, I am," I replied firmly. "Those borders were drawn by a pencil anyway."

Sensing opportunity, Tudjman pushed me for more concessions. "When will you withdraw the Serbian troops from . . ." as he mentioned a location I had never heard of. "Where is that?" I asked Ted Olic, who had been raised in Serbia and was slated to join my cabinet. "You must be kidding us," Tudjman said mockingly. "Mr. President"—Olic addressed Tudjman directly—"you should know that Mr. Panic left Yugoslavia a long time ago. He really has no idea."

"These details are unimportant," I said impatiently. I was more than willing to recognize all of Tito's administrative boundaries as international frontiers and to agree that my government had no territorial claims on Croatia. I strongly believed in the federal system that worked so well in America, and I had a clear view of European integration. In 1992, the Treaty of Maastricht had only been signed a few months earlier, but I already considered a borderless, free trade zone on the European continent to be a veritable fait accompli. "Look, Germany and France were great enemies, but today there is practically no border between them," I reminded the Croatian strongman. Even at the height of a brutal civil war, I saw this type of regional integration as a matter of destiny for the Balkans. I spoke frequently of my desire for a "United

States of the Balkans," and I could never understand these endless debates over land and borders, when the ultimate goal, to my mind, should be reconciliation and entry into the European Union.

While I knew friendship or reconciliation was probably too much to ask for, I pleaded with Tudjman on the need to reach a partnership, decrease tensions, and seek an end to the war in Bosnia. But Tudjman had his own nationalist agenda and aspirations in Bosnia. For all the flexibility that I tried to show, I simply could not engage him or find any type of common ground.

This was mystifying and maddening to me. I had never encountered supposedly responsible people so impervious to reasoned argument and seemingly so indifferent to human suffering. I had put myself out on a limb and had been met only with stoic, uninterested responses. This went further than my being untrained in diplomacy. I now realized I was dealing with a group of individuals far different from those I confronted in the business world. There, individuals sought compromise, solutions that benefited everyone. For Tudjman and others, politics was a zero-sum game. There were winners and there were losers.

Before departing, I decided to take the initiative in another way, by using the only weapon left to me—the news media. I would have to go over the heads of the diplomats and politicians. After my meetings, I was confronted by a slew of microphones, cameras, and reporters. Admittedly, it could have gone better. I broke my glasses as I sat down and was working to fix them while at the same time parrying with reporters—alternating between joking and upbraiding. I would stand up and sit down. To make a point more forcefully, I raised my voice. I accidentally called myself Yugoslavia's president, when I meant to say prime minister. To watch the video now, I must concede, is to see a man untrained and unprepared for the klieg light intensity of press scrutiny.

Nonetheless, I stated in no uncertain terms that I was prepared to recognize Bosnia as an independent and sovereign state—provided it guaranteed equal political, civic, and human rights to all of its people. I said that I was willing to end support for the Bosnian Serbs and stop the war. The reporters were incredulous, and many were openly skeptical that I could accomplish all that I promised. According to one reporter, "We were just laughing at Panic. He seemed really out of his depth." A subsequent editorial in the *Washington Post* accused me of being Milosevic's Trojan horse and a Serb apologist who had "crashed" the party in Helsinki.

I refused to be intimidated, however. I repeatedly reminded the reporters that under the constitution, I as prime minister was responsible for the conduct of foreign affairs. "I am like the president of the United States, and Milosevic is like governor of California," I said. "If he gets in my way," I said several times, "God help him." Milosevic phoned me upon my return to Belgrade. "Milan, why did you have to say such a thing about me?" he whined. "Why did you have to say it over and over again that 'If he gets in my way, God help him.' You know, Milan, that is not the way to talk." "But I meant it, Slobo," I laughed. Milosevic, his innate insecurity raging within, was less amused.

On July 14, 1992, I was officially sworn in as Yugoslavia's prime minister. In my acceptance speech before the Yugoslavia parliament, I stunned the assembled guests by speaking in the language of peace and reconciliation—not age-old slights—and promising to actively seek peace with the country's breakaway republics. I feel I was a breath of fresh air in the turgid political atmosphere of Belgrade. I shocked the parliament with a dramatic plan for peace, promising to withdraw Yugoslav army weapons from Bosnia, calling for a cease-fire in the embattled state, and pledging to end ethnic cleansing, which I called "the disgrace of our nation."

I also declared "respect" for the national aspirations of our neighbors and pledged to begin negotiations on the recognition of Slovenia, Croatia, Macedonia, and most controversially, Bosnia and Herzegovina. "Other countries have recognized these states," I said. "Who are we not to recognize them?" As Milosevic sat stone-faced in the first row of the parliament, I even expressed support for self-determination among ethnic Albanians residing in Kosovo. The speech was praised across the political spectrum. Said one observer, "He was the only politician with real authority in Serbia to stand up and publicly denounce the Bosnian Serb army and volunteers for their disgraceful atrocities in Bosnia/Herzegovina."

Having officially accepted the job, I now set up shop in the Yugoslav government building, a cavernous structure of glass and concrete overlooking the Danube and a symbolic reminder of the nation's once grandiose ambitions. Built in the 1950s when Tito aspired to turn Yugoslavia into an important player on the world stage, it featured vast reception halls and offices and was adorned with huge tapestries and sculptures by artists from across Yugoslavia's former six republics. My office was the size of a basketball court, its anteroom bigger than the Oval Office. And it was here, in this relic of past glory and thwarted dreams, that I sought to run a country in the throes of collapse.

By 1992, Yugoslavia was a shell of its former self. Reduced to only two republics, Serbia and Montenegro, the nation was dominated by Milosevic's Serbian republic fiefdom. Still, I feel I made an extraordinary effort to bring some vitality to the federal government, in order to serve as a potential counterweight to Serbia. To that end, I brought in a series of reformers and young technocrats who shared my enthusiasm for bringing political change.

My limited knowledge of the local political scene was an immediate problem. I retained the defense portfolio and enlisted Tibory Varady, an ethnic Hungarian who taught law at Belgrade University, as minister of justice after Vojislav Kostunica, a constitutional lawyer and leader of a small political party, turned down the offer.

My choice of Dr. Ljubisa Rakic to be foreign minister proved contentious. An old friend whom I had met in the early 1980s when Rakic was doing research at UCLA, Rakic was an outspoken regime critic, and Milosevic objected vigorously to the choice. "If you take Rakic into the cabinet, we will bring down your government," he told me. I stood firm. Milosevic then offered a compromise. He would tolerate Rakic inside the cabinet if I took two Milosevic allies and named one of them, Vladislav Jovanovic, foreign minister. I reluctantly agreed—then appointed Rakic deputy prime minister and made him the head of a ministerial foreign affairs committee, and as such superior to Jovanovic. I want to make it clear that the foreign minister is not a creator of foreign policy, I told Jovanovic, but the executor of the policies set by the committee.

As it turned out, making my cabinet choices was the easy part—divining the intent of the bureaucracy was something else altogether. Much to my dismay, Yugoslavia seemed to be governed by a bizarre law of inertia. It was hard to tell what, if anything, the bureaucracy was actually doing on any given day. I knew that I could not accomplish much without an efficient staff, and so I brought with me a group of Americans to help run the show. Most of the group were ICN employees, whose salaries I paid. They were accorded impressive titles, spacious offices, and large staffs of secretaries and translators.

For the Americans, the transition was a trying one. These were individuals who had spent most of their lives in the world of business, with clear lines of protocol and communication. They found themselves as baffled as I by Belgrade's medieval procedures and outdated infrastructure. Worse, the bureaucracy was completely unaccountable. The Americans could discern no lines of authority or any serious fiscal and administrative discipline. To the government's native bureaucrats, these were positive features: They knew the sources and levers of power, however arcane, and acted accordingly. Things only started to get better when many of the Americans began to recognize the almost mythic respect with which rubber stamps were held. Signatures meant nothing. Each of my assistants had his or her own rubber stamp made. They were soon delighted by its hidden powers, and marveled at the doors it opened.

The Americans formed a zone of comfort around me. Their business-minded, goal-oriented efficiency served as a necessary counterweight to the Balkan addiction to interminable oratory. Whenever I had my Serb countrymen consider an issue, they invariably would talk the whole thing into oblivion and nothing would get done. I hoped that an efficient, well-run and uncorrupted government might help to change the culture of suspicion and mistrust that so many Serbs rightfully had toward their leaders.

My longtime personal assistant, Marcia O'Hagan, ran my office with her usual alacrity. She brought in a plane-load of office equipment, pencil sharpeners, filing cabinets, computers, and fax machines. Another ICN employee, Deborah Levy, assisted her in running the battery of local secretaries who still sharpened pencils with knives and pulled staples out with their nails. The Serbian Americans in my group, including Olic, were given more sensitive positions because they knew the local language. Others were given key jobs in my security detail.

David Calef was brought over and became our de facto propaganda czar. Like many of the Americans, Calef was initially unimpressed with Serbia. Despite pockets of ancient beauty, Belgrade seemed ugly to him. It was as if, he once put it, its rulers had dedicated themselves to defining the lower limit of bad taste. But after a while, his views evolved. The country, he discovered, was made magical by its people and its atmosphere of mystery. At the personal level, the people were warm, the connections instant. Calef discovered that personal relationships were essential and that discussions always went better in the bar or over lunch. He was used to conducting his business at his desk, but Serbs used their offices as phone booths and did their business in cafes.

I hoped that Americans like David could inject a new dynamism into the government and set an example for the bureaucracy. "We tried to raise the work ethic in the government," Calef said. "All of us were at work at eight o'clock, no matter what had transpired the previous evening. We hoped by way of example and exhortation to get things moving. No more let's stop and have a smoke in the canteen." I led the way. I was up at daybreak, and worked as hard and as long as I ever had at ICN. The bureaucracy was shaken to have a prime minister at his desk first thing in the morning, demanding reports and issuing directives.

As a newcomer to Serbian politics, I leaned heavily on Scanlan, who became my chief advisor on both foreign and domestic matters. Jack was particularly crucial, as I often found myself obsessed by feelings of inadequacy. "I didn't know anything about the job," I told him years later. Moreover, I was prone to make diplomatic faux pas whenever my friend was not around. To take just one example, during a visit to Paris, French president Francois Mitterrand and I agreed in principle to re-open air travel between Belgrade and Paris, despite UN sanctions preventing such a move. I was asked about it during a press conference, but instead of seizing the opportunity to announce that France was ready to break ranks, I deferred to Mitterrand, who smoothly side-stepped the question. I should have exploited the opportunity, but I did not.

I had far more problems than simply inexperience. It took less than two weeks for my security people to discover that the Serbian leader was listening to all our conversations. They discovered eavesdropping devices on the phone lines in my office. I was also surrounded by policemen who were reporting the goings-on inside my office and residence. Milosevic knew about cabinet decisions even before we announced them. As a result, I summoned my American staff to the garden of my residence. "I want you to assume that every conversation that you are having is being monitored," I said, "regardless of where you are in our hotel rooms, offices, everywhere."

I decided that all of my key people except Scanlan should move into the prime minister's villa. In retrospect, this put an even greater burden on the staff as their workload doubled. The daily government business transactions, cabinet sessions, and meetings with individual ministers, planners, and delegations tended to take place at 7:00 p.m. or later. After dinner at the residence, the real working day began. The residence itself, considerably smaller than my Pasadena mansion, was swept for listening devices. While none were found, here, too, my staff and I were surrounded by butlers, maids, cooks, gardeners, drivers, and messengers, all of whom we believed could be susceptible to secret police pressures.

Yet, for all these distractions, I continued to run the government as best I could. I maintained declaratory powers, which I used liberally. I could change a policy simply by making an announcement, giving an interview, or issuing a statement—even though implementation was uncertain. And beyond the drumfire of daily crisis, I believe I emerged increasingly as the leader the Serbian people looked to.

Even inside the bureaucracy, the mood was beginning to change. Balkan bureaucrats tend to go with the winner, and I looked like I might just be the one. As defense minister in my own government, I took special care in massaging the generals. I never knew when I might have to rely on them in a pinch. One day while visiting the Batajnica military air field outside the capital, I tried to make my best impression on them. I knew from my early experiences that, in the Balkans, personal courage and skill in handling weapons go a long way. On the spur of the moment, I decided to take a spin in a MiG-29 fighter jet. I enjoyed flying and, many years earlier, had learned to pilot an aircraft. There was something quite extraordinary about racing the heavy machine down a runway and getting it into the air; the takeoffs gave me a sense of invincibility—an unusual emotion during those heady days.

But, of course, what goes up must come down.

6

SEARCHING FOR HELP

While I had growing confidence about my performance in Belgrade, I still felt a debilitating lack of credibility in the international arena. I knew that my ultimate success in ending the war in Bosnia and bringing real political change to Serbia would depend largely on international support. On my own in Serbia, I could not hope to depose Milosevic if he decided not to honor our arrangement. So I increasingly sought support from other major countries. There was no other way for me to be taken seriously, Scanlan argued. "You've got to meet world leaders and convince them of your sincerity," Jack told me. "You need to establish your credibility."

The day after my official swearing-in as prime minister, I flew to Paris to meet with Francois Mitterrand. Both cordial and supportive, the French president told me that the upcoming international conference on Yugoslavia in London would be crucial to my efforts. That forum, Mitterrand offered, would help to garner support for my political program despite American recalcitrance. Britain had just assumed the chairmanship of the European Community, so, while I was still in Mitterrand's Elysee Palace office, I placed a call to John Major, the United Kingdom's prime minister. Major was unavailable, and I was transferred to Quentin Hogg, the number two in the Foreign Office. Hogg casually mentioned that British foreign secretary Douglas Hurd would soon be coming to Belgrade for his first visit to the country—and he would be meeting with Milosevic.

I was livid. Hurd was meeting Milosevic and had not even bothered to tell me, much less arrange a meeting. I told Hogg that Hurd was welcome provided he found time to meet with the prime minister of the country. That was impossible, Hogg said. The trip had been planned before I had become prime minister. Moreover, the British believed that to meet with me would confer some measure of legitimacy on the Federal Republic of Yugoslavia, which most of Europe did not recognize. I was beside myself. How could the British be so short-sighted? Didn't they realize that a visit from Hurd would only confer more legitimacy on Milosevic, the man who was most responsible for the Balkans' unending cycle of violence?

Infuriated, I told Hogg, "Mr. Hurd can come only under the condition I just outlined. Otherwise I will instruct the military to turn his airplane back. I will order the army to prevent his aircraft from landing at the airport. Milosevic is finished with foreign affairs. You've talked to him, and it only brought more bloodshed. I am offering peace." Flying home, I remained steadfast. If the British wanted to undermine me, I would fight back. Nonetheless, the incident put us in a gloomy mood.

After several days of diplomatic back and forth, Hurd relented. He would call on me at the presidential suite at the Intercontinental Regency Hotel, but not in the prime minister's office. Hurd was unwilling to recognize my role as the prime minister of a rump Yugoslavia. The next day we met and had a warm if perfunctory meeting. Afterward at a press conference, journalists asked why Hurd was negotiating with Milosevic, who had no constitutional responsibility for foreign affairs. Hurd was long on reasonable opacities and optimism, but short on substance.

Most frustrating, however, was the lack of backing that I was receiving from the United States. Increasingly, U.S. policy was taking an arms-length approach to the Balkans. At the end of July, I rushed home to California to be with my wife Sally, who had suddenly fallen ill. During a stopover in New York, I met with UN secretary-general Boutros Boutros-Ghali and four of the five permanent members of the UN Security Council. The American ambassador to the UN refused to meet with me.

On July 23, I wrote a personal letter to President George H. W. Bush asking for help, which was not acknowledged. I then tried to arrange a meeting with Eagleburger in Washington. (Only days later, James Baker resigned his post to run Bush's reelection effort, and Eagleburger was named his replacement.) Eagleburger instead relayed an acid and patronizing message through his old colleague Scanlan: "Jack, I want to make sure you get this message clear to Panic. I don't want him to come to Washington tomorrow, so that there would be no impression that we back the deal of swapping Milosevic's removal for the lifting of sanctions. Baker is not going to negotiate this. He cannot. This is a matter for the United Nations. Tell him please not to question my friendship. This is not a matter of friendship. I feel I am his friend, but he is in the big leagues now. That's the way it is."

I decided to fly to Washington anyway in the hopes of convincing Eagleburger to meet with me. Jack and I pulled into the private aviation terminal at Dulles airport, and, with the help of Maryland congresswoman Helen Delich Bentley, arranged for a conference call with the new secretary of state. Bentley was from a Serb-American family and a strong supporter of mine. "Larry, let's sit down and talk about it," I said. "Can I come and see you?" "Absolutely not," Eagleburger responded. "Well, surely we can sit down as friends, have a bottle of beer. Surely we can do that," I asked. Eagleburger said he was under strict instructions. "I couldn't have a glass of beer with you even if you were my grandmother," he added. "But Milan needs your help," Bentley interjected. "Why not have him explain things to you directly?" "No," said Eagleburger.

Frustrated and dispirited by the slight, I dispatched my deputy prime minister Rakic to Washington to meet with Eagleburger instead. They were old friends, and Eagleburger warmly embraced the doctor, whom he called his Serbian brother. Rakic told him that we wanted to rid his country of Milosevic and the Communists, but the Americans were hampering the effort by undermining me and, thus, bolstering Milosevic. "You've got to help us. We are the first noncommunist government in Yugoslavia since 1945." Despite their personal closeness, Eagleburger was blunt. "You are only a decoration, you are a smokescreen," he replied.

When Rakic reported his conversation with Eagleburger, I felt an extraordinary sense of frustration. On how many fronts could I fight? I thought I understood the fundamental problem of Serbia, Croatia, and Bosnia and I wanted to solve it. But I was continually confronted by the polite, guarded faces of international officials who had a tenuous knowledge of the area, and whose dealings were ensuring Milosevic's survival, not his downfall. I found something dark and dubious about the whole situation.

The Western diplomats were always quick with the cliché that the Balkans are the powder keg of Europe. Yet, I began to feel that they were providing the powder, and these little countries were merely the kegs. Rebuffed by the United States again, I decided to take Mitterrand's advice instead. I would try to use the upcoming London Conference as an opportunity to demonstrate that I was in charge in Belgrade, and to help put the collective pressure of the international community on Milosevic.

And so I began another whirlwind tour of European capitals to build support for the conference. My hope was to gauge international views on the Balkan situation, but even more importantly, to establish myself as a credible political leader. At one point, I told reporters, "Just talking about peace can help bring peace." First I traveled to Geneva to meet with Croatian officials regarding a swap of war prisoners. Then I was off to London, where I met with John Major—who briefly forgot my name at a press conference only hours after the meeting. Next came Hungary, back to Yugoslavia, and then Bulgaria, Romania, and Macedonia. This was followed by trips to Greece and Albania and, finally, Turkey, a key supporter of the Bosnian Muslims. I hoped the Turks would relay my position to Bosnian president Izetbegovic before he got to Sarajevo on August 13.

Several months earlier, I had written to Izetbegovic offering to cooperate with him on a long-term peaceful solution to the Bosnian conflict. Though he met with me briefly in July, this time Izetbegovic refused, even going so far as to dismiss me publicly as a clown. As I soon discovered, the Muslim leader was not interested in compromise or reconciliation. From my perspective, Bosnian politicians had to bear some of the responsibility for the dissolution of Bosnia. But I never had the sense that they were seeking or even desired reconciliation with their neighbors. They wanted to win the war, and they wanted the West to provide the political and military support. Winners and losers. A zero-sum game.

To be sure, I had no illusions about the actions of my Serbian brethren. All three sides must bear blame for the unending cycle of violence and war. Still, I was particularly incensed by the West's attitude toward Croatia. Tudjman, the leader of Croatia, was no better than Milosevic, and just as willing to engage in ethnic cleansing and use civilians as pawns in his own political games. But getting that message across to Western policy makers was virtually impossible.

Soon, I would find myself face-to-face with the ongoing tragedy in Bosnia. While flying to Sarajevo from Belgrade, I received a note from my security personnel warning me of a likely assassination attempt on my life. I passed it along to ABC News reporter Sam Donaldson, who was accompanying me for the visit. I was unafraid—this was not the first time I had received such threats. I even joked that if this was my day to die, then so be it. I refused my staff's pleadings to wear a flak jacket for the drive from the Sarajevo airport into the city. Donaldson's producer, David Kaplan, was impressed with my moxie and said to me, "If you're not wearing one, I'm not going to wear one either." It was a fateful decision, and one I feel terrible about to this day. Donaldson and I were safely lodged in an armored personal carrier while Kaplan and other journalists rode behind. Sure enough, at the spot where my staff had warned of a possible attack, a sniper bullet felled Kaplan, killing him instantly.

When we arrived in Sarajevo, I was informed of the tragedy. I was crushed and could not help but feel personally responsible. When confronted by the journalists, I let loose. In an emotional outburst, I described all Yugoslav leaders as criminals and racists. I accused the journalists present of reporting this war in an unprofessional manner. However justified at the time, these flashes of impetuous, impolitic behavior quickly fed into the official gossip already circulating about me. Some claimed that my public grandstanding was endangering the lives of those around me. Others called me mercurial, a maverick, tactless, impulsive, unpredictable, intransigent, a lightweight.

Things became so difficult that even routine travel became a problem. On the way to attend a Brussels meeting, my aircraft, which also carried a group of international journalists, including Sam Donaldson, approached Austrian air space. The pilot told me we would have to turn back. "We just got a directive from an Austrian air controller that they cannot allow us to fly over Austrian air space. We need special clearance." I asked to talk to the Austrian air controller. "This is Prime Minister Milan Panic of Yugoslavia. I am formally requesting that you give us clearance." The voice over the radio was uncertain. "Sorry sir. I am not authorized to speak to a prime minister." I responded, "We are on our way to make peace and you better get clearance in the next three minutes or there is going to be the biggest international diplomatic scandal you've ever seen." "I am going to have to get clearance from our prime minister," the controller said. "You have three minutes!" I warned him. Two minutes later, the controller responded, "Mr. Prime Minister, you have clearance to proceed."

Another incident occurred after I reached Brussels. The outgoing European Community negotiator for Yugoslavia, Lord Carrington, initially refused to talk to me, but finally relented, agreeing to a short meeting. The scion of a great English noble family, Carrington looked and acted the part, and was known for his casual combination of wit, erudition, and carefree elegance. He was also thoughtful and considerate, and worked diligently to resolve the Bosnian conflict. "Nice to meet you, Mr. Panic, presumably prime minister," Carrington greeted me, possibly without malice. I took it as a calculated insult. "Nice to meet you, presumably lord," I replied, without missing a beat. This was an inauspicious opening for a meeting that ended up producing little. I was angry with myself for being so direct and undiplomatic. In retrospect, the pressure was getting to me.

By myself in Belgrade, far from my home and family, I began suffering unprecedented bouts of pessimism and self-doubt. I wondered if maybe the critics were right. Maybe I had bitten off more than I could chew. I began to fear that I was destined to fail in my efforts. Cosic had once joked with me, "You've got money and I've got glory, so what are we doing in politics?" It was a thought that plagued me.

Throughout these tiring summer months, even as I was trying to establish myself, Milosevic was drifting along on the political waters, taking cover behind silence and dodging questions about his voluntary departure. It was clear to all concerned that he no longer had any intention of keeping his side of the bargain. For all my troubles, my ratings in public opinion polls were soaring. My approval rating was around 80 percent while Milosevic's ratings were plummeting. Even Milosevic's grip on the media was weakening. The cover of the national weekly magazine NIN, once firmly in his corner, was emblazoned with the headline: *Milosevic—"Fear"; Panic—"Hope."*

Inside the entrenched Communist bureaucracy, where Milosevic had residual support, the mood toward me was also changing. Some key members of the old Communist elite, who had initially dismissed me as an inconsequential figure, now were discreetly offering their assistance. Milosevic has to go, they agreed, but how remained the question. Together with Cosic, I discussed working to unseat the Serbian strongman. Time and again, I told Cosic, I had tried to get Milosevic to resign, and time and again Milosevic had dodged the issue. The country was heading to disaster. The time had come for a decisive action.

Cosic was prepared to have the Serbian president arrested. But Cosic also feared that a coup attempt would risk a civil war in Serbia, where Milosevic still had supporters. Another, potentially more bloodless option we considered would be to have Cosic run against Milosevic in the December elections for Serbian president. Cosic's nationalist credentials were impeccable and, combined with his literary fame, he was virtually certain to beat Milosevic. Both of us were confident we would win. But, with Milosevic, one could never be positive that he would accept the results. Even as we became more inclined to follow the electoral path to Milosevic's removal, I was unsure Cosic and I had opted for the right course. The idea of a quick, bloodless coup began to prey on my mind. Was it technically feasible? I consulted with Olic. "What are you going to do with him?" Olic asked. "Place him under house arrest? And then what?" He recommended that I sound out the key military commanders.

The next morning, after a tennis match with my regular partner, the chief of staff General Zivota Panic (no relation), I mentioned that I had a serious issue to discuss. Sensing what might be afoot, the general recommended we go to Karadjordjevo, Tito's old hunting lodge outside Belgrade. While taking a walk through the forest, I swore the general to secrecy before broaching the subject. Milosevic, I said, had become a millstone around Serbia's neck. He must be removed. "But I don't want any bloodshed."

The general appeared slightly shaken. "That could be done," he said, after a long pause. "You could arrange to pick him up while he is having a late-night drink at my house," I offered. General Panic's tone was grave. "Yes, we have no choice," he said. "It can be done. You go to Washington and get support for us. If you tell me everything is okay, I'll do it." I was relieved. Later that day, I inspected the four thousand-strong elite presidential guard, which served under the command of Cosic.

But although I never had a hard time making a decision when it involved business, I began to waver once again. I abhor violence. I had pleaded for the lives of German soldiers during my days as a partisan. And now I was contemplating an action that was bound to lead to more violence, and even death. Suddenly, I found myself horrified by the banality of my own scheming. My usual common sense and strong streak of pacifism had suddenly abandoned me. What had happened to that other Milan, who had dreamed about a political and economic renaissance in Yugoslavia?

After further reflection, I became convinced that a coup d'état could lead to significant violence in the country, particularly among Milosevic loyalists who might feel they had nothing to lose. I was also worried about the likely lack of U.S. support for the coup. I couldn't be sure that the United States would recognize a new government or embrace a change in leadership. And without international backing, I was concerned that the whole effort could fall apart—and risk putting my life and that of my staff at risk. On top of everything else, I decided that it was simply the wrong thing to do.

On the surface, the relationship between Milosevic and me seemed undisturbed. In fact, Milosevic, who lived a block away, was a frequent visitor at my residence. Milosevic was a funny guy in that way. He never went out in the streets, never went to a restaurant. But he loved to come to the villa and talk to me. I continued to raise the issue of resignation. I reminded Milosevic that he was in a line of work in which there was no pension plan and hardly any possibility of peaceful retirement. "I am offering you a graceful way out," I reminded him, "you have agreed to leave." But each time, Milosevic found a way to avoid the issue.

One evening in mid-August, Milosevic arrived unannounced at my residence. We chatted a bit in the living room before moving out onto the spacious veranda that overlooked the city below. The sky was lit up by the reddish orange of a setting sun. I had drinks brought—wine for me, whiskey for Milosevic. Serbia needed a dramatic change, I began to argue for the umpteenth time. Milosevic had to resign, for the sake of the country. I kept laying into him: "The people who are guiding you into this mess are not your friends," I told him. "You are responsible for what is happening in Bosnia. You are responsible for the catastrophic economic conditions in Serbia. Resign, Slobodan! If you don't do it, there will be war for many years, and many more people will get killed."

When I get going like this, I can't stop. When you believe something emotionally, intellectually you become a powerhouse, even if you really aren't. The dictator listened. He seemed to be struck dumb by the audacity and passion of my argument. He looked puzzled and alarmed. Already, my brief exposure to high diplomacy had taught me that in each public persona was a smaller, stranger person, who bore little resemblance to the one millions saw on television screens. On this night, it seemed truer than ever.

Milosevic was a man with a very limited range of facial expressions. He constantly kept his inner feelings in check. His face gave nothing away—it was that of a natural actor who would look someone straight in the eye as he lied to them. But at this moment the dictator appeared to me as small, shattered, and depressed. "Why are you going after me like this?" Milosevic finally asked me. "Because you lied to me! You agreed you'd resign," I responded. Then things really started getting out of control. He looked at me and said, "Enough." I have never seen him so despondent. He took a revolver—he often carried one—and tried to hand it to me. "Shoot me," he said. "Get it over with." I was stunned, I couldn't believe my ears. "Are you crazy?" I cried. "Do it," Milosevic said. I wondered what had made him go careening off in this loony direction. Part of me thought Milosevic was serious. After all, both of his parents had committed suicide. "You've got to be sick!" I screamed at him. "You have children, you have a family. You want me to shoot you? You are sick. Resign! That's what I want you to do. Stop doing this wrong thing!" I began to seriously believe I was dealing with a madman.

Milosevic put the gun down and sank into his chair. We drank without speaking for a while, until at last Milosevic stood up, belched, and said, "I have to go home." I sat alone on the veranda. Obviously I'd heard rumors about Milosevic's deep depressions. They circulated for months. Street demonstrators had chanted slogans, calling on him to follow his parents, a reference to their suicides. In leadership meetings, his mood regularly oscillated between elation and reticence. I wondered if the incident that evening was another of Milosevic's tricks. Perhaps the revolver was not loaded?

A few days later, I arranged to have lunch with Milosevic in the president's office. The meeting lasted several hours and was our last. I repeated my offer to arrange for a dignified exit for Milosevic. "You must step down for the sake of Serbia," I told him yet again. "You don't understand what I mean to Serbia," Milosevic replied. "I'm the Ayatollah Khomeini of Serbia. The Serbs will follow me no matter what!" I was stunned. "How can you say something so stupid?" I replied angrily.

The dictator said nothing for a long while. "Milan, you don't understand!" he told me. "You work for me! Don't you realize it?" The dictator was now scowling at me, assuming his public face with the tightened lips and cast-iron features. "That's even more stupid than you being Ayatollah Khomeini!" I cried. "You are crazy! We are adversaries!"

When I again pressed him to resign, Milosevic bluntly stated that he had no intention of doing so. "But we have an agreement!" I bellowed. Milosevic snorted. "What agreement?" He looked me in the eye and repeated the statement with absolute conviction. "Let's call in Mitevic," I cried. "He is your friend and is a witness." Mitevic was sitting down to dinner when a phone call summoned him urgently to Milosevic's office. A car was already on its way to pick him up.

Mitevic appeared within minutes, looking visibly frightened. We must have looked a bit flushed. In front of us were bottles of whiskey and wine. "I immediately saw that the president and the prime minister had argued, and I assumed they were both drunk," he recalled later. I immediately accosted him. "Now Dusan, tell him about the agreement"—stressing the word agreement to indicate I was talking about the document Mitevic and Scanlan had drafted, and that Milosevic and I had verbally approved in Mitevic's presence.

"Is there any such agreement?" Milosevic asked acidly. Looking at the dictator's scowling face, Mitevic hesitated, wondering if his professional future, not to mention his life, might be in danger. "Yes," he replied. He began perspiring profusely. He looked like he wished he could disappear into thin air. Mitevic knew well Milosevic's vengeful streak. "You see," I turned triumphantly to Milosevic. "There's your witness!" "Did I sign it?" Milosevic asked. "No," Mitevic replied, truthfully. "So you see"—Milosevic looked at me with a flash of sardonic humor—"that's a worthless piece of paper!" Mitevic was dismissed. As he was leaving, Milosevic and I were still throwing ugly epithets at each other behind closed doors.

A few weeks later, he was fired. For all our many disagreements over the years, I will always remember how, at that moment of testing, Mitevic risked his job—and even possibly his life—to speak the truth to Slobodan Milosevic. It was the right thing to do, and it took enormous courage.

7

BATTLING THE PAST

Before departing for Yugoslavia in July 1992, I sat down for an interview with the *Los Angeles Times*. In it, I noted that, "Like most Americans, I don't think about the past, but the future. I have adopted that philosophy and will apply it to Yugoslavia." For a country and a region mired in the past, it was and remains a radical concept. And for all of my efforts to impart "an American view" on my countrymen, I often found myself at war not simply with Milosevic and his henchmen, but with the burdens of history.

Soon after I became prime minister, my deputy, Dr. Ljubislav Rakic, and I met with Radovan Karadzic, leader of the Bosnian Serbs, and told him that all offensive operations in Bosnia had to stop. Karadzic broke into an apocalyptic tirade about Serbian mythology. "We have been waiting for eight hundred years to solve the Serb question," he ranted. "It cannot be solved without a world war." "Let's wait another eight hundred years," Dr. Rakic injected, acidly, "but let's stop the war." Karadzic's face twisted in disgust.

Karadzic was not alone. Within weeks of my return to Belgrade, I had met dozens of nationalist politicians and cultural figures who seemed highly intelligent and well-versed in the history and culture of Serbia. Yet, they were filled with a startling level of gloomy exoticism and vicious xenophobia. They carried with them the various national traumas—the Turkish yoke, Austrian and German imperialism, and the Croatian genocide of World War II—as if they were badges of honor,

and all were used as historical justifications for the evil now being perpetrated in the name of Serbian nationalism.

If anything, since the outbreak of fighting in Bosnia-Herzegovina in
March 1992, the acts of violence there had only become more severe
and repressive. Regular reports of civilian massacres and atrocities were
being aired in the West, while most Serbs were oblivious to the carnage.
And for all the many historical grievances that Serbian nationalists ru-
minated on at length, this time the Serbs were not the blameless victims. They were the oppressors who had ignited the fuse by resorting to
violence.

I had never dealt with such people before, even in my youth. The
people I met were seemingly in love with the idea of victimhood. They
insisted that the world must recognize Serbia's wounds and suffering
and apologize. In America, didn't General Sherman burn down Atlanta? Milosevic's leading philosopher, Mihajlo Markovic, argued publicly
as he defended the wars in Croatia and Bosnia. I was aghast by the
parallel. Yes, Sherman burned Atlanta, and then he turned his army
eastward to torch the plantations of the Southern aristocracy and the
public buildings of the Confederacy. But Sherman also freed more than
forty thousand slaves. His goal wasn't wanton destruction and murder
for its own sake—it was to destroy the infrastructure that had fueled the
Confederate struggle against the North. How could anyone, I wondered, compare the struggle to abolish slavery with ethnic cleansing and
indiscriminate revenge killings?

To be sure, I was not immune to the pull of nationalism. I grew up,
as most Serbs did, steeped in the country's culture and history, from the
awful Kosovo massacre and four centuries of servitude to the long independence struggle and the terrible, destructive wars that followed. Yet,
I also came from a school of thought and background that viewed Serbian nationalism in a far wider context. Like many in the larger cities,
my family had viewed Serb nationalism as a component of a larger
Yugoslav idea, the idea promoted by Serbs as well as other southern
Slavs (Croats and Slovenes) who lived under the Habsburg Empire.

Generations before, a large segment of the educated classes in Serbia had enthusiastically accepted this view as a genuine feature of Serbia's modernization, along with the ideas of individual liberty, political
democracy, respect for the rule of law, human rights, and cultural free-
doms. True, these were Western ideas, not indigenously Balkan con-

cepts. Yet Serbia had embraced many of them in the nineteenth century. The country introduced a parliamentary system, a modicum of local
self-government, due process, and respect for individual rights. This
was also my vision for Serbia, fueled by my belief in the American way.
I imagined a future Yugoslavia with a constitutional democracy; a system of checks and balances; civilian control of the police; and, most
fundamentally, pluralism, respect for diversity and opposing points of
view, and political powers contesting for and transferring power based
on free, democratic elections.

But men like Karadzic had a vastly different view of the future.
Karadzic was born in a small village in northern Montenegro. There,
countless generations were imbued with a coldly nationalist idea,
sprung from the epics and old ballads whose seemingly soothing lyrics
fostered extremism, moralism, and a self-righteous air. Karadzic and his
followers were in love with Serbia's exotic past; with her painful pro-
logue. The Serbs are God-chosen people, they argued, and God is a
Serb.

Nothing angered me more than the argument, often used as an
excuse for inaction by the West, that the southern Slavs were fated to
do battle with each other. War was not preordained. It relied on the
malevolence and machinations of leaders such as Milosevic, as well as
Tudjman and Izetbegovic, for whom the past served the purposes of the
dictator. Milosevic alluded to Serbian notions of historical inadequacy
time and time again, and he did so in a way that resonated in Serbian
villages and small towns. In Milosevic's gloomy and paranoid worldview, outsiders were conspiring against Serbia. There was no room for
dissent, no room for the weak of heart who counseled conciliation and
diplomacy. In short, there was little room for a worldview like mine.

While Milosevic and his cohorts trolled in the past, I worked tirelessly to introduce the politics of modernity into Serbian life. I wanted my
countrymen to paint over history, blot out the disturbing parts, and
think only of the future. California had put a brand on me for life. I was
amazed at the political culture of Serbia and its appetite for reveling in
ancient slights. How, I wondered, could millions of people seem so
easily brainwashed by a dictator? But then I met some of the regime's
leading intellectuals, poets, and novelists, whose chauvinism and jingo-
ism seem to cast a magic spell over the collective consciousness.

No one figure embodied that power of the past more than Dr. Vojislav Seselj, the baby-faced leader of the ultranationalist Radical Party.
Milosevic once described him as the politician he admired most. Seselj
strutted about in fatigues, a pistol stuck in his belt, accompanied by
menacing-looking bodyguards. He was intelligent, well-educated, and a
master of political invective. He spoke with a revivalist fervor that left
meeting halls ringing with cheers. He once publicly urged his followers
to use rusty spoons to gouge out the eyes of their Croatian and Muslim
enemies.

Listening to tirades by politicians like Seselj, I at times felt I was
surrounded by madmen. Rather than leading a nation transfixed by the
idea of being special and different, I wanted Serbia to be nothing more
than ordinary. Serbia would never move beyond its bloody past until it
became just another part of the modern world. I am a liberal, politically, but I strongly believed that in Serbia government was the problem,
not the solution. I hoped that by privatizing the economy, I could de-
centralize the nation and take some of the power away from the government elite.

In my business dealings, I had a simple motto: You can't let history
get in the way of the future. I have always believed in dismissing personal resentments and quarrels to move toward profitable solutions.
But this mind-set seemed anathema to many I spoke with in the
government. In Serbia, patriotism equals supreme sacrifice. The only
patriotic act a Serb can perform is to die for his country. To survive is
almost like being a coward. This was the mind-set I wanted to break.
No sacred Serbian myth was too great for me to attack, even Tsar Lazar.
At one point during a heated parliamentary debate, I said about the
famed fourteenth-century battle, "This was a stupid fight. How can you
glorify a defeat?" I told a stunned parliament: "You people here are not
just fighting the Turks; you are fighting the whole world. I will not
accept that! We are not going to fight the world! We are going to make
peace."

Rarely if ever had a Serbian politician uttered such blasphemous
ideas. When jeers rose from the audience, I picked up a glass of water
and yelled, "You don't think I'm a fighting Serb? Then I'll throw this
glass in your face." The deputies were now more bemused than an-
noyed. Many began to laugh, and some even congratulated me. I was
pleased with my performance. In an article headlined "Yugoslav-

American in Belgrade Leads Serbs Who Won't Follow," the *New York Times* reported me saying, "They need shock therapy. They are living in Disneyland." But that minor victory aside, I was fighting an uphill battle. Changing the direction of an entrenched bureaucracy and a centuries-old political culture, all the while seeking peace, was a Herculean task. "It was like trying to fix your carburetor while continuing to drive your car," as David Calef well put it.

This deadly confluence of mythology and history came into clear focus in August. I had heard the stories of Serbian atrocities in Bosnia. On cable television, I saw the flight of Bosnian Muslims—bedraggled unfortunates lugging small children and their meager possessions as they trudged to transit camps near the Hungarian border. The disturbing images of men and women who had forfeited everything, their homes and their past lives, awaiting resettlement, reminded me of my own past—when I was a young man in an Austrian transit camp for refugees near Salzburg in August 1955. I remembered being ashamed at the feeling of helplessness and my complete reliance on strangers for handouts.

On a whim, I ordered a helicopter to take me to the refugee transit camp at Lake Palic, near the Hungarian border. I knew the moment I entered the tent city that the reports about the crimes in Bosnia were true. The atmosphere was unusually subdued as I walked from tent to tent. I saw the cowed and ailing old men. They were clearly terrified, and the look on their faces dramatized the awful, terrible things their eyes had seen. Many seemed too afraid to show any emotion at all. I fought to keep my own rising emotions in check. On the flight back to Belgrade, I realized that I must do everything to stop this horrible war—not simply for the Bosnian Muslims, but for my own people. I must break the spell of history and show the Serbs a path to a more hopeful future. I had been given an extraordinary opportunity to end suffering and to bring hope to a nation. I vowed to myself once again not to fail.

The road to peace ran through the United Kingdom. The London Conference on the Former Yugoslavia in August 1992, was, in retrospect, one of the high points of my political life. For the first time, I felt that I was beginning to acquire a greater sense of my own political identity and a growing understanding of governance. I prepared for the event as if I were going to do battle—which in many ways I was. I was determined to impress upon a skeptical international community that I was not a puppet of Milosevic—that I was my own man. While success would mean both a personal and political triumph, failure would gravely damage my credibility in Yugoslavia. Considering the fact that many of the conferees didn't even want me to come, the stakes could hardly have been higher.

In a letter to Chinese ambassador Li Daoyu, the rotating president of the UN Security Council, I outlined my political program in detail. My government was opposed to the use of force. We accepted Tito's borders, had no territorial claims on any former Yugoslav republic (I specifically mentioned Bosnia and Croatia), rejected ethnic cleansing, pledged full cooperation with any international investigation of human rights violations, promised to urgently eliminate repression and human rights abuses in Kosovo, and pledged cooperation in ensuring humanitarian aid to Bosnia and assisting refugees in returning to their homes. I also renewed my request for UN monitors on all border crossing points between Bosnia and Serbia, as well as the stationing of UN observers at all Yugoslav military airfields.

In effect, I pledged to give the West everything it wanted, but the diplomats, too savvy and cynical by half, could not help looking the gift horse in the mouth. In the weeks preceding the conference, the British organizers continued to insist on having Milosevic participate as a member of the Yugoslav delegation. Scanlan, in London on a delicate mission to resolve the problem and tethered with strict instructions from me, negotiated with Quentin Hogg. But Hogg insisted that the Europeans wanted to talk with Milosevic. He was still seen as the region's only true power broker. Jack reminded Hogg that the Yugoslav constitution accords the prime minister the sole responsibility for the conduct of foreign affairs. Moreover, by dealing with Milosevic, Jack pointed out, Western allies were only strengthening him as a player on the world stage. All working with Milosevic did was undercut my position, and undermine the political groups in Serbia dedicated to the dictator's overthrow.

But the British were not prepared to concede, and, frustrated, I had little choice but to relent. Instead, I decided to make the best of a bad situation. When Milosevic asked to speak, I scribbled a note and handed it to him. "Shut up," it said. Later, when the conference chairman, British prime minister John Major, called on Milosevic to address the plenary session, I vigorously opposed it. "You speak when I tell you to speak," I told Milosevic. Then, turning to Major, I added: "This is my delegation and I will speak for my delegation. If I think Mr. Milosevic should speak, I'll tell him to speak."

Milosevic was stunned. So were the international diplomats. Nobody had ever said such things to Milosevic in the presence of other people, let alone at a gathering of world leaders. Self-effacement was for Milosevic the most unnatural of roles, yet he remained mum. Those who were aware of his proclivity for revenge knew that this was the beginning of open war between us.

Having effectively grabbed the microphone from Milosevic, I spoke passionately of peace. "Some participants at this conference still have agendas that bear the potential for fueling the flames of a broader conflict rather than furthering the quest for peace," I said. "I am not one of them. I do not speak for Greater Serbia. I speak for greater peace." I was beginning to hit my stride. I believed that reconciliation between Serbs and Croats was essential for repairing Yugoslavia's troubles. They were the two biggest bullies on the block and, until they resolved issues, there would be little hope for progress. As a result, I announced that I was prepared to recognize Croatia and its borders, provided the Serb minority was guaranteed full political and cultural rights.

My proposals shaped the conference agenda and its conclusions. The final document addressed all the issues of concern to the international community: no use of force; acceptance of Tito's borders; no territorial claims; recognition of all new states provided the rights of minorities were guaranteed (this included a commitment to respect Bosnia's prewar borders). In addition, the UN declared its intention to send peacekeepers to Bosnia. Milosevic actually pledged to follow the twelve-point package, despite his reservations on the second point dealing with the acceptance of Tito's internal borders.

At last, I was being taken seriously by international powers. I held bilateral talks with the foreign ministers of France, Russia, China, and Britain, who seemed begrudgingly willing to grant me a level of respect. Only Eagleburger struck an inauspicious tone. In Scanlan's view, his old friend was maintaining an air of purposeful hostility. "I did not seek him out," Jack said, "and he went out of his way to stay at the other side of the table. We asked for a meeting but Eagleburger's executive assistant,

William Montgomery, told me Eagleburger is 'under instructions not to meet with you.'"

A humiliated Milosevic was already long gone from the proceedings. He left in a huff, and without informing anyone that he was taking one of the Yugoslav government's two aircraft. He and his advisors didn't even bother to settle their hotel bills, which I paid with my credit card. For Milosevic, my behavior in London was the final straw. It was clear that the man he had brought into Belgrade to serve as a smiling, American face for his government could not be reined in. Milosevic would brook no further abuse. I had to go. Immediately.

Upon his return to the Yugoslav capital, Milosevic convened his closest allies, led by security czar Radmilo Bogdanovic, at a meeting at his weekend home in Pozarevac. The main role was assigned to Vojislav Seselj of the Radical Party, whom Milosevic frequently used as a tool against his domestic critics. Milosevic urged his allies to launch a no-confidence motion against me in parliament. Sixty-eight deputies accused me of betrayal and charged I had exceeded my mandate in London. Specifically, they cited my concessions on Kosovo and my willingness to accept Serbia's border as established by Tito, even though that left sizable Serbian minorities in Bosnia and Croatia.

With the die cast, Milosevic's allies went on the offensive, spreading rumors about my incompetence and accusing me of "selling out" at the London conference. They said I was an "adventurer" who "knows more about California than about Kosovo." The nationalistic rhetoric quickly assumed an anti-American tone and focused on Scanlan, who was portrayed as the "dark figure" in an American plan to destroy Yugoslavia. "One former American ambassador was orchestrating things on one side of the table while the other former American ambassador [Eagleburger] was doing the same on the other side of the table," Seselj alleged.

I was hardly in the mood to compromise or relent on my peace aims. I fiercely defended my antiwar policy. I told parliament, "I am the man who will negotiate and negotiate and negotiate until the doors are closed, and even then I will try to open them." Appearing on local Belgrade television, I denounced Milosevic's conduct of the Bosnian war. "Yugoslav citizens have two choices," I said. "One is peace, the other is tragedy."

As was often his habit in emergencies, Milosevic summoned a group of his most loyal constituents—Kosovo Serbs—to stage demonstrations against me in Belgrade. But this time Milosevic overplayed his hand. Public opinion polls showed my approval rating at 82 percent. More ominous, from Milosevic's point of view, were threats of mass demonstrations by Belgrade University students. And worst of all for him, he didn't have the votes to back his effort. The Yugoslav parliament's Montenegrin contingent announced their support for me and openly attacked Milosevic's tactics. "All these parliamentary maneuvers call to mind the atmosphere of lynching," said Montenegro's leader, Svetozar Marovic. Opposition leaders called on the people to take to the streets and oppose the move. The motion to remove me formally died when President Cosic forcefully endorsed me and called the parliamentary vote "ill-considered and politically damaging." My removal, he added with emphasis, would imperil Serbia's very survival.

For several months Cosic and I had been moving closer together—both ideologically and personally. I have extraordinary respect for extraordinary people, and as an intellectual and famous author, Cosic was just such a man. Though our backgrounds could not have been more different—I was a rich businessman, Cosic a rumpled intellectual—we made an effective team. We shared the same goal: end Serbia's isolation and rid the nation of Milosevic. What must have been most galling for Milosevic was that he had brought us together, and now we were plotting his downfall.

Confronted by his increasingly confident and popular adversaries, Milosevic knew he was defeated for the moment. He tried to distance himself from the parliamentary move, with a terse statement issued by his Socialist Party announcing that its deputies would not support their own motion. Milosevic aides even spread rumors that he had nothing to do with the no-confidence effort. An embarrassed parliament overwhelmingly endorsed the results of the London conference: 13 deputies against, 115 in support of my plan for peace.

I sensed a political opening, and announced that I would demand Milosevic's resignation if he attempted to obstruct the peace policies agreed to in London. "We must dismiss the entire old team that has conducted Yugoslav policy so far," I told my aides. "They have lost every game. People must realize that lying is finished, joking is over, there has been enough deceit." "I am through with him," I said of Milosevic in an interview with the *New York Times*. "We are on a collision course."

To demonstrate my resolve, I abruptly fired Foreign Minister Jovanovic, Milosevic's most loyal ally in my government. I then turned against an even more important Milosevic henchman—First Deputy Interior Minister Mihaly Kertes, who was in charge of the federal secret police. Kertes, an ethnic Hungarian, was among a handful of individuals who had access to the dictator's home and was trusted by the dictator's wife, Mirjana Markovic. Kertes and another deputy police minister, Radovan Stojicic-Badza, had supervised "ethnic cleansing" and other covert operations in Bosnia and Serbia.

When it was reported that minority groups had been the target of organized harassment, forced expulsion, and murder in the Serb region of Vojvodina, I explicitly banned the violence and ordered the police to act forcefully in putting an end to it. But when I discovered that it was continuing unabated, I asked Scanlan what could be done. "Well you can fire Kertes," Jack told me. "I can fire him?" I responded incredulously. "Sure," said Scanlan. "You're the prime minister of Yugoslavia." And with that, Kertes was gone.

The removal of these key officials was a shot across the bow for Milosevic. It sent signals through the military and police establishment that he was able to control neither me nor the political direction of the country, and that his power was waning. Sensing his grip on Serbia was in danger of being fatally undermined, Milosevic ended his silence and shrilly blasted my foreign policy as "harmful to Yugoslavia." He declared that I was a puppet of the Americans, who were scheming to weaken the Serbs. But unfortunately, and as the world would soon discover, the United States was far from being in my hip pocket.

As was so often the case during my tenure as prime minister, once I had put out one fire, another inevitably appeared. This time it was diplomatic discussions about expelling the country from the United Nations. Yugoslavia had been a charter member of the UN, but when the country was broken up into five separate countries, each new nation was admitted to the world body with its own flag. It was a point of pride to Milosevic that he had kept not only the name Yugoslavia for the territory under his control but also the title to its membership in international organizations, including the United Nations. "It was an important concept for him," recalled Ilija Djukic, the shrewd and experienced new foreign minister. "To him, it meant that he salvaged what could be salvaged from Yugoslavia. The others had destroyed it, not he. He had saved Yugoslavia."

I thought this was a largely cosmetic matter—the entire issue seemed like a tempest in a teapot. I had said as much to Boutros Boutros-Ghali, when the UN secretary-general had warned during our previous meeting in late July, "don't insist on continuity" for Yugoslavia. But given Milosevic's complete intransigence on the issue, I wanted to do everything possible to avoid a major confrontation. Hoping to enlist support from Beijing and Moscow, I flew to China to meet Li Peng and arranged to meet Boris Yeltsin during a stopover in Russia. Peng and I were old friends, having met several years earlier when ICN was exploring the possibility of expanding its pharmaceutical business to China. Foreign Minister Qen Qichen, a former ambassador to Belgrade and fluent in Serbo-Croatian, was also an old friend of Djukic, the new foreign minister.

The China visit was a splendid ceremonial occasion. Thousands cheered my motorcade. An exquisite state banquet was held in the Forbidden City, followed by a visit to the Great Wall and fruitful discussions with Premier Li Peng and Qen. But the warmth and courtesy I was accorded notwithstanding, I was rebuffed on the central issue of my political agenda. China refused to exercise its Security Council veto to prevent the issue of Yugoslavia's expulsion from reaching the floor of the General Assembly, or to force the lifting of sanctions on the Belgrade government. "Mister Panic," Li Peng said, "we are under sanctions too. Don't you understand that? We are fighting our own problems, so please don't ask us to veto things in the Security Council."

While Sally, who had flown from California to join me, and I were touring a new industrial complex in Tienjin, I received an urgent diplomatic message from the Russian ambassador, Igor Rogachev. The situation at the United Nations was evolving, Rogachev said. Moscow expected the Muslim nations to prevail on the issue of expulsion. Russian president Boris Yeltsin was now urging the prime minister to abandon the current position and seek admission to the UN as other former Yugoslav republics had done.

The message was repeated by Russian foreign minister Andrei Kozyrev when he met me in Moscow on September 16. Kozyrev also assured me that such a move would help Moscow head off the expulsion drive.

So I relented. Soon, Kozyrev and I were mobbed by journalists who demanded to know whether Yugoslavia would insist on its right to retain the original UN seat, and whether Moscow would veto an effort to bring the expulsion vote to the General Assembly. "I have an important announcement to make," I said. "We shall submit a request for membership in the UN."

When the news reached Belgrade, Milosevic issued a statement declaring that my decision was neither legal nor binding. I was once again in a tough spot—to me, the UN issue was a red herring that distracted the international community from the more important steps that needed to be taken in order to bring peace. But at the same time, as the prime minister of Yugoslavia, I was hesitant to accept defeat. Besides, why was the international community focusing on Yugoslavia's UN seat when I was putting forward a real plan for peace? Why not give me the international support I needed, instead of giving Milosevic yet another phantom issue to use for increasing his own domestic support? I found the arcane machinations of international diplomacy mind-numbing.

I knew I was playing with a weak hand. I had lost the Chinese and Russians, so I made a last-ditch effort to bring the United States to my side. Deputy Prime Minister Rakic—who was still the only person in the Yugoslav government who could get a meeting with Eagleburger—went to Washington. The secretary once again warmly embraced his "Serbian brother," but refused to yield on the expulsion issue. "You've got to give us a signal of support," Rakic pleaded. "We can't do it," the secretary replied.

Eagleburger offered a curious insight into the administration's thinking. The move to expel Yugoslavia was being pushed by a bloc of Muslim nations. "I'm your friend," Eagleburger told Rakic. "But you have to understand that, in the past twenty years, America has established a bad record in the Islamic world. We are seen as being against Islamic fundamentalists, Libya, the PLO, etc. We need to be seen as supporting moderate Islamic countries such as Turkey, Albania, and Bosnia."

On September 21, in a final effort to stave off the drive for expulsion, I came to New York for the opening of the United Nations General Assembly, with plans to speak to that body. The permanent members of the Security Council apparently were worried that I might disrupt the proceedings. So they invited me to a meeting at the Russian mission with their foreign ministers and their UN ambassadors. At this meeting,

Scanlan, who had accompanied me, and his once close friend Eagleburger found themselves on opposite sides of the table. Eagleburger, seemingly lost in thought and shuffling his papers, looked up at Scanlan with what seemed like a moment of clarity. "Jack, five years ago, would you have thought that you and I would be sitting here in these respective positions," he said in a low and serious voice. "No," Jack replied. There was never again to be so much as a gleam of the old friendship between the two.

I tried to place the United States on the defensive. I reminded Eagleburger I had done everything in my power to comply with all of Secretary of State Baker's demands in Helsinki: I extended diplomatic recognition to Slovenia, offered to settle disputes over Serbia's border with Macedonia, had begun dialogues with Kosovo Albanians and the Croatian government, pledged to work for peace in Bosnia, offered to allow UN monitors to Serbian airfields, and the list went on. "If you give me your support, I could do more and accomplish more," I implored them. It was time, I argued, for the West to do something concrete to help me in my pursuit of peace. Although I am generally a poor public speaker, I feel I made a masterful presentation at that time, reeling off facts and figures and tying everything together into a forceful argument.

"Panic was brilliant," Jack said later. "He was convincing, and I thought he was at the edge of turning things around." I made it as clear as I could that peace was my priority, and that I had been making headway in Serbia in spite of the Western nations' refusal to support me, or even to formally recognize my government. "All except Eagleburger were beginning to be swayed by him," Scanlan recalled. "But Larry was tired. This was an evening meeting. He sat in the middle of the table opposite us and he placed his walking stick on the table. Then he took the floor and said, 'Now let's recognize where we are. We have a resolution that has been adopted, which calls for the suspension of Yugoslavia's membership. It doesn't impose any new sanctions; it doesn't impose any new programs. The Muslim governments want us to go beyond this. They are putting on lots of pressure, and they have support from many Third World countries. So if we deviate from what we have agreed to, we are going to have a problem and the outcome would be worse. We don't want to reopen that.'"

Eagleburger's statement basically ended the discussion. Even at the time, I understood that this was a near fatal assault on the bright hopes of my government. In fact, it was a double blow for me: Not only had I been undermined by the West once again, but Milosevic had been given a huge symbolic victory, which he could now use to burnish his nationalist credentials.

Still, I hoped to at least salvage something from the meeting. "Okay, we'll accept this," I told the group, recognizing the inevitable, "but we are still going to make our case tomorrow. But I want something from each one of you. I want each one of you to give me fifteen minutes of verbal support after this meeting." The ministers agreed. Outside, the street in front of the Russian Mission was swarming with journalists. The five ministers came out to make statements to the press, each speaking warmly about my government. Even the normally cantankerous Eagleburger briefly noted my "constructive role" in the process, and the efforts I was making on behalf of peace.

The next day, wearing a dark blue suit, white shirt, and a red tie with white stripes, I stepped to the podium of the General Assembly. I knew the cause was lost, but I tried to appear confident and in control. I criticized UN debates that focused on politics rather than on ways to achieve peace in the Balkans. I reminded the Assembly that I had unsuccessfully asked for UN monitors to be deployed "at our airfields and at our borders" to control the flow of arms, and that I had at London proposed several thousand UN troops be placed on the Yugoslav-Bosnian border. "I renew that request now," I added. "We still have some militant nationalists who defy our orders. We need your help. Please come as peacemakers. My only goal is to restore peace and stability in the Balkans. Do not undermine men of peace and peace-loving Yugoslavs."

In allowing the stationing of foreign soldiers, I was agreeing to surrender a key element of Serbian sovereignty—all in the pursuit of peace. I also, I believe, exposed the double standard that was being imposed on my country. While there were no Yugoslav troops deployed in Bosnia anymore, I noted, a recent *New York Times* article reported that ten thousand regular Croatian army troops were fighting there. "Yet Croatia sits in your midst, not subject to criticism and sanctions," I said, even as the assembly was about to vote on Yugoslavia's expulsion.

I went on to condemn ethnic cleansing as "horrible, unacceptable and unforgivable" and vowed to help the refugees return to their homes. I brought up my own personal experiences—my wife was a Roman Catholic, and one of my daughters had married a Muslim and converted to that faith. "Your acceptance of the transformation we are seeking, and your recognition, would further the cause of peace. Your rejection, I fear, would impair it." It was a passionate appeal, but a failure. Against a steady background of bad news—reports of continued fighting in Bosnia, ethnic cleansing, massacres, rapes, Serb-run concentration camps, and Muslim refugees flooding into Western Europe—127 nations voted in favor of expulsion. Only five African nations voted with Yugoslavia against the motion.

I believe this loss at the United Nations reflected once again the extraordinary bind I was facing as a leader. I had a plan for peace, but I simply could not convince my adopted country, the United States, to provide the support I so desperately needed, no matter how many times I implored them. In fact, two days after this defeat in New York, I finally got the one-on-one meeting with Eagleburger that I been seeking since my first day on the job. We met at the Willard Hotel in Washington, and were joined by Scanlan and Congresswoman Bentley. I felt like a supplicant, and begged Eagleburger for at least a token gesture of support.

"I did what you wanted me to do," I reminded Eagleburger. "I didn't make a fuss at the UN. Now I need something. I can't go back empty-handed. How about some easing of the sanctions like providing fuel oil for hospitals and schools? If the United States says yes, others would go along." "I think we can support that," Eagleburger said. Congresswoman Bentley chimed in, "Larry, he needs our backing." "Milan, how much support do you have in Yugoslavia?" the secretary asked. "Look at the polls!" I cried, reciting the latest figures that showed me to be the most popular political figure in Serbia. For the first time, Eagleburger offered a grudging note of support, indicating that, while they could not be in the lead on the issue, they were willing to lend some backing.

Jack Scanlan came away from the luncheon believing that Eagleburger was finally coming around to our view. "When he said, 'I think we can support that,'" Scanlan said, "I thought Eagleburger would not have said that unless he believed the administration was behind him." My aides and I also began a campaign to get congressional support. Scores of letters were dispatched to prominent figures. I called on several key congressional leaders, including Senate Minority Leader Robert Dole, who had become something of a spokesman for the anti-Serb lobby in Washington.

Ted Olic, who attended the Dole meeting, said the senator had no real grasp of the situation and depended almost entirely on notes prepared by his staff. Ironically, his key staffer was Mira Barata, daughter of a Croatian immigrant who had been in the same German refugee camp with me in 1955–1956. "Dole walked in and said 'I'm the most hated man in Serbia,'" Olic recalled, as if it were a point of pride. Things quickly went downhill from there.

I didn't know what to make of it. It was like talking to a brick wall. Dole asked me to intervene on behalf of an Albanian woman who feared she would be expelled from her apartment in Pristina. He insisted I should prevent that. I obviously wasn't aware of this purported Pristina crisis, and couldn't help but ask whether she had paid her rent. Dole said he did not know. I was flabbergasted. Here I was trying to move the peace process forward—and get rid of Milosevic—and all Dole could talk about was one woman in Pristina!

Even as the congressional offensive stalled, Eagleburger, not surprisingly and true to form, began to backtrack. A confidential letter to me, dated September 25 (the day after our meeting), was patronizing in tone and, among other things, chastised me for making a critical remark about Ambassador Zimmermann. That same month, Eagleburger made his true feelings on the Balkan crisis known in public. "I have said this 38,000 times, and I have to say this to the people of this country as well," said Eagleburger, in a moment of rare candor. "This tragedy is not something that can be settled from outside, and it's about damn well time that everybody understood that. Until the Bosnians, Serbs and Croats decide to stop killing each other, there is nothing the outside world can do about it." In an October 4 interview with the *Los Angeles Times*, I lamented this fatalistic attitude from Washington. "The lack of support from the United States is chipping my power away, along with the possibility of democratization of Yugoslavia." Days later in a *Philadelphia Inquirer* interview, I argued again for outside assistance. "If I don't get support from the outside world," I stated simply, "I won't succeed."

Nothing better dramatized the gap between U.S. policy and my program than the situation in Kosovo. In the postwar period, the Kosovo region, largely populated by Albanians with a sizable minority of Serbs, had gradually gained a measure of autonomy within Yugoslavia. As that happened, anti-Serb policies, actions, and violence had encouraged a Serb migration and an influx of Albanians from elsewhere in the country. In 1989, however, Milosevic abolished the region's independence and imposed a harsh, Serb-led regime, under which Albanians were purged from jobs, schools closed, and dissenters jailed. I realized that any peaceful settlement of the Balkan conflict that did not return to Kosovo some form of political and economic autonomy was doomed to failure. This would be a very tough issue. But, as I told my aides, there is no issue on which a compromise cannot be found—even one as seemingly intractable as this—provided both sides respected each other's interests.

I had earlier extended feelers to Kosovo's ethnic Albanian leaders. I offered to meet with them (a significant concession from a Serbian leader) and told them I would grant the province complete autonomy within Yugoslavia, provided they abandon their demands for secession. On October 14, shortly after thousands of Albanians had fought tear gas battles with baton-wielding Serb police, my education minister went to Kosovo to meet with local leaders in an effort to restore Albanian-language education in primary and secondary schools.

The next day, I myself flew to Kosovo for talks with Ibrahim Rugova, leader of the Albanian opposition. Rugova was a gentle and sophisticated poet whose signature was a woolen scarf he wore even on the hottest summer day. Determined to win him over, I publicly embraced the Albanian leader and endorsed all Albanian demands except secession. Once again, I was prepared to take on all of his country's sacred cows in the pursuit of peace. "Dr. Rugova and I are going to democratize the Yugoslav system," I declared. I publicly berated Serb nationalist militants who wielded power in the province since Milosevic imposed virtual martial law in 1990. Rugova was more guarded. "Mr. Panic agreed to lift all the discriminatory laws," he said, "and I am grateful for that."

In private talks, I urged the Albanians, who comprised 90 percent of Kosovo's 2.1 million people, to take part in the political process in order to defeat Milosevic in the forthcoming elections. The solid Albanian bloc of nearly nine hundred thousand votes, I pointed out, would prove decisive. But, for Rugova, the ghosts of the past obstructed the promise of the future. Fearing another Serbian trick, he remained noncommittal. All Rugova was prepared to do was make a procedural concession in the direction of compromise—he agreed to a joint task force to study legislation, education, and other contentious issues.

I again appealed to Washington for help, asking the administration to nudge the Kosovo Albanians along and get them to join the democratic opposition in an effort to oust Milosevic. "In seeking to redress the legitimate human rights grievances of Kosovo Albanians," I wrote to Eagleburger, "my government faces strong opposition from solidly entrenched political elements in Serbia. If you wish to help us do the things that are right and necessary to do in Kosovo, I must ask you to use your good offices to urge the Albanian leaders to participate in the political life of Serbia and Yugoslavia via the electoral process. I need their participation in the elections later this year if we are to have any real hope of electing a truly representative parliament. . . . If the Kosovo Albanians opt out of our political process by failing to participate in our elections, it will undermine my government's efforts to right the wrongs of the past."

But Eagleburger continued to throw roadblocks in the way. I was flabbergasted. Even this simple lift—encouraging the Albanians in Kosovo to take part in the political affairs of their country—was too much for the Americans. In another letter I asked Eagleburger for "all possible assistance" by American nongovernmental organizations and other bodies to help organize a free election in Yugoslavia. I also asked Eagleburger to permit the shipment of television equipment designed to extend the range of a small independent TV station and thus break Milosevic's stranglehold on TV news. Even that paltry request was refused.

Taking another tack, I returned to Kosovo prepared to make a dramatic announcement of the restoration of autonomy to the province, on the pattern of Tito's "limited sovereignty." All I needed was Rugova's nod. But Rugova rebuffed me. I was accompanied on the trip by the cochairmen of the London Conference on the Former Yugoslavia: Cyrus Vance, who represented the UN, and David Owen, soon to become Lord Owen, a former British foreign secretary who represented the European Union. Owen and Vance also tried to sway the Albanian leader. "We begged him to reconsider," Owen said. "But he was in a secessionist mood. The Albanians were not interested in the future of Yugoslavia."

Three days after my fateful meeting with Rugova, Eagleburger finally responded to my earlier offer. He again said that it was imperative for Serbia to cease all oppression in Kosovo, renounce the use of force there, and restore Kosovo's autonomy—all steps I had already pledged to make. "Finally," Eagleburger added, "I would like you to be aware that we are encouraging Rugova and other Albanian leaders in Kosovo to urge their people to participate in elections which meet international standards." All well and good—but Eagleburger's letter was dated October 31, three days after Rugova had firmly and finally rejected my overture. Eagleburger made no mention of the equipment permits for the independent TV station.

With this taste of what I had been putting up with my entire tenure in office, the EU's David Owen blasted Washington. "The cravenness in dealing with this issue," he said, "the bureaucratic tangle of sanctions and the gutlessness with which we were dealing was appalling." This whole episode, to me, was another in a long list of missed opportunities—by Rugova and the Kosovars and, most appallingly, by a United States government that seemed inclined to do everything possible to make my job that much more difficult.

Even so, I was not ready to quit. "You have to be an optimist," I would tell my dispirited staff. "Show me a good loser and I'll show you a real loser." But even as I tried to rally my exhausted troops in further pursuit of peace, Milosevic plotted to get rid of me once and for all.

8

COUP D'ÉTAT IN BELGRADE

In the spring of 1992, I must have seemed to Slobodan Milosevic the perfect foil—a California businessman with excellent political connections, I could smooth relations with the West and help to lift international sanctions against Yugoslavia. Six months later, it was clear to Milosevic that he had badly misread both me and the United States. I had zero support in a Republican-dominated Washington—if anything, my relationship with the U.S. government was now marked by animosity and indifference. Not only was I not going to improve relations with the West, but I was becoming increasingly recalcitrant and difficult to control. As such, Milosevic concluded that he would face little opposition from the United States if he took what he considered to be much-needed action against me.

By October 1992, it was also clear to Milosevic that going after me would not be enough. He would also have to unseat his former spiritual mentor, Dobrica Cosic. Once an ideological supporter and fierce advocate for Serbian nationalism, Cosic had since seen the dangers of aggressive Serbian chauvinism, and slowly came to realize that Milosevic was doing nothing but harm to his beloved Serbia. Together, he and I had become identified with the various anti-Milosevic forces in the country—a coalition of opposition parties, students, intellectuals, disgruntled technocrats, and Yugoslav army officers.

Milosevic struck quickly against us. On October 9, 1992, he arranged an interview on Belgrade television to publicize his conflict with Cosic and me. The interviewer was the new director general of Radio Television Belgrade, Milorad Vucelic, an intelligent and thoroughly cynical Socialist politician with an impressive talent for lying. In the course of this bizarre interview, Milosevic asserted that I was clearly controlled "from Washington"—a charge that ran against every piece of available evidence. Ominously, he said of Cosic, "it remains to be seen" who controlled him. In addition, Milosevic played the nationalist trump card yet again—blasting any idea of compromise on the Kosovo issue and the very notion of peaceful negotiations between Serbs and Albanians. This, Milosevic affirmed, is "absolutely out of the question. I could never support such a thing."

Cosic responded by publicly calling on Milosevic to quit, blaming the dictator for both the Bosnian war and Serbia's deepening international isolation. "If my resignation was discussed as much at home and abroad as Milosevic's," Cosic told the daily *Politika* on October 15, "I would step down." Verifying that the divide between the two men was now unbridgeable, Cosic stated that "Milosevic and I differ essentially in the understanding of democracy and ways of pulling the country from the abyss in which we find ourselves." In another interview, with the *Washington Post*, Cosic noted that in the past the world had offered Serbia a choice of slave or grave. But, this time was different: "Neither capitulation nor war, neither a slave nor a grave. Survival is in peace, and this can only come through a new policy that is far-sighted and imaginative."

As Cosic's words resonated throughout Serbia, Milosevic prepared his response. While both Cosic and I were in Geneva attending one of the countless international meetings about the crisis in the former Yugoslavia, the perfect opportunity arose for Milosevic's next move. This particular session had actually made some headway—an agreement was reached to reopen telephone, road, and railway links between the Serbian and Croatian capitals—and I was eager to fly back to Belgrade while Cosic remained in Geneva. But on Saturday night, October 19—at the same time my Boeing 727 was taking off from Geneva—Milosevic's police carried out what amounted to a virtual coup d'état.

Under the pretext that they were returning night photographic equipment borrowed from the federal secret police, Milosevic's agents tricked an unsuspecting duty officer to open the steel doors of the secret police headquarters. Heavily armed and masked police units were soon inside the building. They proceeded to lock out the building's employees and then systematically removed all secret police files and hauled them to the Serbian Interior Ministry, which was located across the street. The speed, the secrecy, and the efficiency were breathtaking—particularly considering the general inertia of Serbian bureaucracy. It was all over in a matter of hours.

By the time my plane landed, shortly before midnight in Belgrade, I instantly realized something was wrong—there were no security officials to meet us. "Where are the government limousines for the prime minister's entourage?" my security escort asked. They were all "requisitioned" by the Serbian government, came the answer. "Was this a coup?" Foreign Minister Ilija Djukic recalled asking me. Nobody knew the answer. We moved to the airport's VIP lounge and began working the phones. Jack called Robert Rachmales, the American chargé d'affaires, at his home. Rachmales, who had already gone to sleep, was not aware of any unusual activities in the city. I reached my military chief of staff, General Zivota Panic, at home. The general sounded surprised and professed not to know what was happening. "I am not aware of any crisis situation," he told me. But he immediately promised to check things out and meet me at my residence at 1:00 a.m.

We rushed to my office in a four-car motorcade. Jack went alone in his own car. He wanted to get a clearer picture of what was happening on the ground. Recognizing the severity of the situation, he also wanted to avoid getting snared if a coup attempt was under way. "I wanted to be able to make a run for the U.S. embassy if necessary," he recalled. Jack instructed his driver to keep a distance from the motorcade and to proceed by a circuitous route into Belgrade. But the drive was uneventful. There was little traffic on the road, and it was late enough that the water trucks were already out cleaning the streets. Nonetheless, Scanlan saw the Federal Ministry of Interior building surrounded by police. Across the street, lights were blazing inside the Serbian Ministry of Interior—an almost unheard-of event in the early hours of a Sunday morning in Belgrade.

Jack drove to his apartment and immediately called me. "The federal Ministry of Interior has been seized by police," he said, but there were no other signs of a coup. Meanwhile, the situation in my office was surreal. The foreign minister joked that we should find some playing cards to while away the time. In the early hours of the morning, the commandant of the presidential guards, who were under my direct command, strode into the office with a flourish; he and I conferred alone in the adjacent room. Meanwhile, aides had finally reached the interior minister, Pavle Bulatovic. A proud Montenegrin, he viewed the seizure of his ministry as a blow to his own prestige. He asked me to immediately issue an order to the federal police and the army to retake the building.

Bulatovic's request made me uncomfortable. Ever since my early days as an anti-Nazi partisan, I have abhorred the use of violence. I was deeply committed to solving the problems in Serbia without resorting to bloodshed—if one person had to die to establish my vision of peace and democracy in the Balkans, the project would be a failure. Plus, I thought that if my administration was to be supported by both the West and the public, it could not be marred by a violent coup attempt. I would make my decision, I told my colleagues, after conferring face-to-face with my trusted military chief of staff, General Panic.

When we had earlier discussed using the army to remove Milosevic from power, the general was willing to act. Now, I returned to my residence just before 2:00 a.m. to find General Panic and fourteen of his key generals—all in full uniform—waiting in the living room. Their presence added to the sense of danger felt by the American staff, who had retired to the upstairs bedrooms. Calef thought their faces were shadowed by malice and by caution. "We thought we were going to wind up in jail," he recalled.

"Do you have any guns here?" my Serbian American security man, Dimitri Vukcevic, asked Marcia O'Hagan, my personal assistant. "Only a revolver," said a terrified O'Hagan. She found a pistol in a closet but wasn't quite sure what to do with it. I spoke with the generals to sort out what had happened. Yes, General Panic said, the federal building had been taken over by the Serbian police. But the whole thing seemed to him like "a tempest in a teapot." The general advised against the use of force. In his view, this was not the best occasion for a confrontation with Milosevic.

I told the general that I agreed with him, and argued that we pursue a legal recourse. "President Cosic agrees," the general said. "I've spoken with him." The next morning, I downplayed the incident and emphasized political and legal remedies for fighting Milosevic. Several of my key aides were dismayed by this approach. "We completely misread the meaning of the takeover," Calef said later. "I told Milan to get rid of this

Panic (foreground), as Yugoslavia's young cycling champion, 1952.

Panic, successful California businessman, 1979.

Allies for democracy: Panic sits in the UN General Assembly with Yugoslav president Dobrica Cosic, 1992.

Prime Minister Panic jousts with reporters, 1992.

Panic makes his case to U.S. secretary of state Lawrence Eagleburger, 1992.

Prime Minister Panic meets with Patriarch Pavle of Serbian Orthodox Church, 1992.

Prime Minister Panic addresses the United Nations General Assembly, September 1992.

Slobodan Milosevic, the hard-line President of Serbia, and Prime Minister Panic fighting back to back: Mr. Milosevic by the means of War and Mr. Panic by the means of Peace.

Political cartoon contrasts competing campaign styles of peacemaker Panic and warmonger Milosevic, 1992.

Candidate Panic speaks to workers, December 1992.

Panic on campaign trail against Slobodan Milosevic, December 1992.

Campaign supporter, December 1992.

Panic casts his ballot for president, December 1992.

Panic talks with President Bill Clinton about potential for peace in former Yugo-slavia, 1995.

Looking for allies: Panic visits the Great Wall of China, September 1992.

guy [General Panic]. I felt we had to respond somehow." Jack Scanlan was even more emphatic. "We are making a serious tactical error," he told me. "I think the general is lying to you." He suspected that General Panic had known about the takeover ahead of time, and that he either colluded to let it happen or was warned off by Milosevic. (I myself trusted the general completely.)

Jack urged that General Panic be fired immediately, and he believed a forceful response was necessary. "You've got to confront this, Milan," he said to me. "You cannot avoid it. This is the ultimate challenge. Of course, it is a 'tempest in a teapot' as far as the building is concerned, but the image of Milosevic blatantly using his police with impunity to seize a federal ministry, and particularly the federal police ministry, will be seen both domestically and internationally as an indication of Milosevic's power and authority vis-à-vis you." But I pushed back, because I did not want to risk bloodshed. Peace is too important, I told him—we will fight this legally.

Milosevic's bold and brazen move had shocked the bureaucracy. But Jack was right about one thing—choosing the path of nonviolence carried political costs. Milosevic had effectively dismembered the federal secret police and replaced it with his own Serbian secret police. At first, the entire episode was deliberately downplayed; there was not a word about it in the press. But we were operating in a city and a government where the most important information was transmitted in whispers. Rumors were floating, and my once unimpeachable reputation was now being undermined. That Milosevic could dismantle the federal secret police overnight, with no explicit response from me, was taken as an omen by many—a sign that the dictator's side would be the winning one when all was said and done.

Calef thought government officials now looked at him differently. "I used to call for a government car to take me wherever I needed to go. Suddenly they said the cars could no longer be used for personal use. But I had no personal life in Belgrade. Everything I did was linked to my job. Then they started telling me, 'Gee you shouldn't really call up for cars, because they know who is calling. You'd better have your secretary call and say it is for somebody else.' Then came the point when they said, 'Americans can't use government cars,' and this simple sentence summed up the changing mood toward Panic."

In fact, the federal government was now in complete limbo. The agreement to reopen road, rail, and telephone communications between Serbia and Croatia on October 24 was simply not implemented. Instead, a convoy of local and foreign journalists that attempted to navigate the Belgrade-Zagreb highway was stopped by armed troops allied with Milosevic. Behind the scenes, Milosevic was regaining ground as his propaganda machine moved into high gear. I was increasingly depicted as enemy to the people and an American stooge. Once again, I found myself in an environment that I didn't understand. I could not believe it. It was like being in a mental asylum where the inmates were running things. Was this politics?

The next blow to my hopes came from my own side. In late October 1992, Cosic called me and asked to meet him at a nearby Belgrade hospital. Cosic, who had already undergone two heart bypass procedures, had just entered the hospital for prostate surgery. He had important news for me: He was bowing out of the race for the Serbian presidency against Milosevic. This was terrible news. The Serbian elections in December were the last best hope for unseating our adversary. I had fully expected Cosic to run against Milosevic and, because of the country's increasingly dire economic situation, Cosic was viewed by most political observers as the presumptive favorite.

I was crushed. My most important political ally was bowing out of a contest that he most certainly could win. Indeed, Milosevic had earlier told the ailing president that he would step aside if Cosic decided to run. "I invited Milosevic on two occasions in September [of 1992] and urged him not to run [in the December elections]," Cosic said later. "I told him I was talking to him like his father—I emphasized the differences in age and experience. Milosevic said he would not run for reelection if I decided to. I'm sure he would not have run had I decided to run." While certainly all of Milosevic's proclamations were to be taken with several grains of salt, it is clear he understood the existential threat that Cosic represented to his continued presidency.

My disappointment was tempered in part by the fact that Cosic believed a grueling political campaign would almost certainly kill him. Nonetheless, his choice to demur could consign thousands, if not millions, of his countrymen to more instability and greater violence. As such, I was furious and begged him to reconsider. "You can sit in the hospital and still win," I insisted. But Cosic would have none of it. This was another grievous blow to my hopes for Yugoslavia, but I refused to hold a grudge even though I was mad. He let me down, but so what?

In any case, with Cosic out, pressure built for me to step in. Indeed, Cosic urged me to take his place, promising full and enthusiastic support. I continued to plead with my friend to reconsider, but without success. While Cosic pleaded ill health, many believed that the situation was far more complicated. When asked later to explain his decision, Cosic was evasive and cryptic. "I thought the situation was odd. I was president of Yugoslavia and I had to resign to run for the presidency of Serbia. This didn't make sense." One can only speculate about the real reasons for Cosic's defection. It's possible that he, too, was intimidated by Milosevic's brazen takeover of the federal security police building. Lord Owen, who met him frequently and liked him, suspected vanity, adding, "I do think that he began to like the trappings of being president of Yugoslavia."

Cosic's decision impacted Owen as well. Still trying to resolve the burgeoning conflict in Bosnia, Owen had come to believe more and more that the only official in Serbia now capable of bringing the fighting to an end was Slobodan Milosevic, not me. "Vance and I were weighing out how much to come out in favor of Panic," Owen recalled later. "We wanted him to do well, but we didn't believe he could win, and we had to somehow keep open the lines of communications to Milosevic. While Cosic was there, we were ready to sacrifice the relationship with Milosevic. Once Cosic bowed out, we had to deal with him." In any case, it probably didn't help matters that Owen wasn't personally fond of me. "He is a bloody difficult person," Owen once said. "He just seemed so mercurial."

Whatever the reason for Cosic's departure, I now found myself in a truly unenviable position. I had never wanted to run for office, and had long ago ruled out political involvement that involved retail campaigning. But now I was facing an unpalatable choice—either run or concede defeat to Milosevic. Given those parameters, I knew that I didn't really have much of a choice at all. I felt responsible for the people who supported my political goals and looked to me for guidance. Most of all, my desire to prevail was almost primal—I was a fighter and wanted to see Milosevic defeated. I told Cosic that if I decided to make the run and was successful, I would stay in office for six months and then go home. "I truly have no political ambitions," I said to him. "I'd like to be known as a person who came back to Yugoslavia to help bring peace and introduce American-style democracy." "Don't tell that to anybody," Cosic laughed. I winced at the reply, as it exposed the gulf between Cosic's vision of Serbian nationalism and my own goals for our homeland. Still, had we continued to work together, I am sure Milosevic would have easily been defeated.

In any event, I wasn't going to move forward without first performing due diligence. I called my old friend Birch Bayh, who recommended contacting Douglas Schoen, a Democratic pollster who had done work for a number of politicians, including Bayh's son Evan, then the governor of Indiana. Schoen is an energetic, resourceful man who was renowned in American political circles for his ability to devise winning campaign strategies, even in the most difficult of political environments. And there were few tougher political environments than Yugoslavia in the fall of 1992.

Answering the call, Schoen came to Belgrade via Hungary (due to UN sanctions, which prohibited direct air travel) and spent two intensive days analyzing the methods and findings of local pollsters. He found their methodology precise and results credible. Their analysis showed I had an almost two-to-one advantage over Milosevic in popularity. In Schoen's view, Milosevic had clearly lost the confidence of the Serbian people, and there was a true hunger for change among the voters. Indeed, according to Schoen, I was probably even more popular than the polls indicated, since citizens of dictatorial societies like Serbia are not typically effusive in their vocal support for opposition politicians. To supplement their findings, Schoen designed his own carefully targeted poll. He would not have the results until after the November 30 deadline for candidates to register for the plebiscite. But even without his own numbers, Schoen was convinced that I could win.

While still debating whether to run, I flew to Geneva for meetings with Cyrus Vance and David Owen. I asked Scanlan and Rakic to join me, and Schoen finagled himself a seat on the plane. I asked Vance and Owen if they could arrange for independent observers to monitor the December balloting and serve as a deterrent to fraud. Vance and Owen would not commit themselves. Instead they asked me to allow international observers into Kosovo. I took the answer (correctly) to mean that they had little interest in the elections, which dealt a further blow to my considerations. If I couldn't rally the West to support me, what protection would I have against Milosevic-inspired fraud? To defeat the dictator, the election would have to be free and fair, and that would mean Vance, Owen, and the West would have to step up.

On the flight back to Belgrade, I sat down with Scanlan, Rakic, and Schoen in my private suite and asked Schoen to present his findings. Harvard-educated Schoen knew very little about Serbia, but he knew a great deal about public opinion polls and the way to shape political campaigns. "Doug convinced Panic that he could beat Milosevic," Scanlan said later. "He said repeatedly, 'I'm a professional, I have talked to everybody else, and I have analyzed other polls. There is no question in my mind that if there is an honest vote you would beat Milosevic.'" "You're at 70 percent, he's at 25," Schoen told me in no uncertain terms. "If you get into this race, I know you're going to win." I wished Schoen could have convinced Owen and Vance of that fact!

Despite Schoen's assurances of victory, there were significant electoral obstacles ahead. I had no political organization on the ground, no campaign manager, no field operation. Even getting on the ballot would be a Herculean challenge. Moreover, I was sure that, without the West closely watching, Milosevic would rig the vote. My political viability in Yugoslavia would be finished and, even worse, I might be the target of an assassination attempt. I peppered Schoen with questions, but the pollster never wavered. "The economy is in shambles," Schoen said. "People don't want war. Milosevic is finished." Finally Calef stepped in and asked me point-blank, "If we get you on the ballot, will you run?" I shrugged. "Yeah, sure." The race was on.

Of course, the decision to run was only half the battle—now my staff had to get me on the ballot. We had a little more than forty-eight hours to gather the ten thousand signatures needed to do that. Calef was put in charge of the petition effort. The first obstacle came quickly—the Serbian election commission provided my office with only one set of forms, with enough space for twenty-eight signatures. So the Xerox machines were put into high gear and petitions were cranked out. Meanwhile, Calef shifted into campaign mode. Hundreds of student volunteers went into action. Working round the clock, they collected more than fifty thousand signatures by the morning of the deadline day. I was stunned, but I remained true to my word. They got me on the ballot, and now I had to do my part.

While Schoen's analysis had given me some hope, at the time I was even more focused on the outcome of the recent presidential elections in the United States. Both Scanlan and I were convinced that, freed from electoral pressures, the Bush administration would finally throw the weight of America behind my campaign. We expected the same from the new American president-elect, Bill Clinton. On December 1, I sent a letter to Eagleburger informing him of my candidacy. No longer pleading for a personal endorsement, I urged the secretary to issue a statement of support for "the Serbian people and democratic forces" in the forthcoming elections. I also asked the secretary of state to provide something tangible for the Serbian people, such as "targeted heating oil aid for twenty hospitals and fifty schools." Finally, I asked that the ban on Yugoslav participation in international sporting events be lifted if the Serbian people opted for a democratic alternative. Granted, it was a token request, but I believed that even the slightest sign of affirmative U.S. support, and the potential for improved ties with the United States, would propel my candidacy forward.

I dispatched similar messages to scores of international figures, ranging from the U.S. Senate's majority leader, George Mitchell, to France's president, Francois Mitterrand. The Serbian people need to know that they had not been abandoned, I wrote. "They need to know that they are not being punished for Milosevic's policies; they need to know that they would be welcomed into the international community if they reject the dictatorship; they need to know that sanctions would be eased."

The response was more of the same, with one notable exception. During my trip to Geneva, I stopped over in Bonn with German chancellor Helmut Kohl. I discussed my possible intentions to seek the Serb presidency. "Mr. Prime Minister, we continue to think that Milosevic holds all the threads of power in his hands. But if you believe in your cause, you must fight for it, just as we fought the Nazis during Hitler's time." I believed deeply in this cause, and in my vision for my homeland. I also well knew that Milosevic would not go down without a fight. It was time to get to work.

9

TAKING ON SLOBO

On December 1, 1992, I stepped before the cameras at Belgrade's Hyatt Regency hotel and announced that I was a candidate for the Serbian presidency. Although local television covered the event, few Serbs were even aware at first that I had joined the race. As Doug Schoen ruefully noted in a postelection article in the *New York Times*, Radio Television Belgrade's thirty-second report of my announcement "dwelled primarily on the fact that the declaration took place at the American-owned Hyatt Regency." Nonetheless, the lack of government media attention did not stop me from offering a withering attack against my opponent. "Milosevic has not kept his promises," I declared. "Our economy is in shambles. Unemployment is skyrocketing. Inflation is out of control. Our children have no future. . . . Under Milosevic we have become isolated internationally and become the victims of crippling sanctions. War rages out of control and yet Milosevic has done nothing. All that he offers is fear, division, and confrontation."

I argued that I would restore hope for Serbia's future through a program of reconciliation and economic recovery. "The forces of division and hatred are arrayed against us. But I'm convinced that we will prevail. The people of Serbia want change. They want a new direction and new leadership. I am convinced that we will succeed only if Slobodan Milosevic is replaced." While the world media supported my move as heroic, the announcement on Yugoslavian TV was followed immediately by an interview with a Milosevic acolyte, who launched a vitriolic personal attack on Jack Scanlan—describing him as a key actor in a deadly American puppet theater whose primary goal was to destroy Serbia.

The fight was now on, and Calef was surprisingly pleased. He enjoyed the grinding schedule of the election campaign. "This is something I related to personally, viscerally," he said. "OK, take the guy head-on." He also loved working with young Serbs. The student volunteers were the most energized people on the campaign. They tirelessly canvassed neighborhoods in Belgrade, plastering cars with stickers and boosting the campaign with their energy and emotion.

Meanwhile, in the Serbian legislature, Milosevic's Socialist Party had surreptitiously slipped residency requirements for the Serbian presidency into an unrelated bill. Not surprisingly, I did not qualify. Milosevic's allies brought the issue to the attention of the Serbian electoral commission and demanded that I be removed from the ballot. Dutifully, the commission played their sycophantic role and declared me ineligible to run in a national election. The decision was immediately appealed to the Supreme Court of Serbia, which—to my great surprise—overturned the ruling and declared that I would stay on the ballot. But even though Schoen had convinced me that the polls showed me ahead, my ability to get my message of *"Promena Sad"* (Change Now) out was hamstrung. The campaign had lost nine precious days, or half the allotted campaign period, fighting the ballot question.

To make matters worse, my campaign had virtually no access to television. I held large, well-attended rallies in many Serbian cities—Novi Sad, Nis, Subotica, Kragujevac, Valjevo, Vrsac, Cacak, Vrnjakca Banja, Krusevac, and finally Belgrade. But Milosevic jealously guarded his monopoly over the only nationwide radio and television network. Each night, vicious personal attacks were broadcast against me. I was portrayed as a CIA agent, an enemy of Serbs, and a tool of the West, sent by the Americans to infiltrate and destroy Serbia. This unremitting tirade of invective deeply concerned me, but Schoen reminded me that our campaign had yet to run its own ads.

Schoen went to work with one of my closest friends from California, Democratic commentator Bill Press, who had had traveled to Belgrade to work on the campaign. Working together, Schoen and Press produced an attack ad that they believed would fatally sink Milosevic. The spot opened with a picture of Milosevic and asked the simple question, "Has he improved the quality of life in the country?" A series of images rolled across the screen, which gave Serbs the obvious answer—long lines for bread and gasoline, shots of ordinary Serbs with looks of quiet desperation. Next the ad cut to an image of me, looking confident and standing on my platform of peace, prosperity, and freedom. Schoen saw the ad as a "knockout punch."

The officials at Belgrade Television saw it differently. They claimed it was too critical. Schoen asked technicians to remove whatever they considered objectionable, and they cut out all the references to Milosevic and even to Marshal Tito. But the TV officials again refused to air it. Press remembers the frustration he and the rest of the campaign staff felt. One more ad showed Milosevic's face and the slogan THEY PROMISED. "Too provocative," they were told. The staff went back and blew up the image so all that was shown were Milosevic's lips. "People would recognize his lips," they were told. Press was exasperated.

They tried again with a commercial that showed a burning match stick with the slogan "The last match for a brighter future, for warmer homes, so that we have light. Vote for Panic." Rejected. And again one of Milosevic with the caption "Offering our children: War, poverty, unemployment, food lines. Vote for a prosperous and democratic Serbia." The verdict always came back the same—"too provocative." For days, the campaign was able to run nothing more than a biographical ad about my career. Making matters worse, the delay in receiving certification of my spot on the ballot meant the campaign would only be able to start running ads on December 10, one week before the campaign officially ended.

Despite it all, my poll numbers remained strong. Milosevic, undoubtedly looking at many of the same polls, unleashed a new barrage of attacks against me. One of the more brazen featured news coverage of a large rally on the plateau in front of St. Mark's Church in Belgrade. There, I was mobbed by well-wishers struggling to shake my hand or just touch me. In a twenty-second segment, Belgrade TV claimed these were scenes of protest demonstrations against me, a "traitor" to the Serbian people and a "CIA agent." There were never any negative signs at any of my rallies in all of Serbia, so the state-run media had to lie. This, of course, was all the handiwork of Milosevic's puppet at the television station, Milorad Vucelic.

One of the most virulent voices against me belonged to a Serbian American woman, Radmila Milentijevic, who was a minister without portfolio in my cabinet—she had been placed there by Milosevic. She denounced me as an unscrupulous adventurer who was bankrolled by the CIA. Forged documents were "produced" to prove the point. This type of blatant propaganda might have been counterproductive in Belgrade, which Milosevic knew he would lose anyway, but his aim was to reach the population outside the capital. Yet, even there, the countryside took to me, extending me an often spectacular and spontaneous welcome. In the town of Krusevac, a seemingly endless crowd of tens of thousands in the central square chanted "Milan, Milan." Calls for "change" repeatedly interrupted my speech. At town hall meetings, lines would stretch out the door as the voters huddled in staircases and hallways to hear me speak.

In the southern city of Nis, which had long been a Milosevic stronghold, I received a thunderous welcome. When my car pulled into the main square, tens of thousands of people were chanting my name. Bill Press later told a U.S. newspaper, "The streets were closed with people just wanting to get a glimpse of him. He was like a rock star or JFK." I soon found myself in front of a growing crowd with no sound system and no stage. Finally, I was escorted to the fourth floor window of a hotel and, with a homemade sound system, could only muster a few words. I told the eager crowd that it was better "that you talk rather than me. You talk and I'll listen." I was blown away by the reception. There was a palpable sense that the Serbian people held a burning, overwhelming desire for change. They wanted an end to war, an end to economic ruin, an end to international isolation, and, most of all, an end to hopelessness. When it came time to go, the crowd rocked our cars and refused to let us leave for more than half an hour.

I drew incredible energy from the fervor of the voters. Yet, at the same time, rumors were swirling that Milosevic's allies were preparing an attempt on my life. Nobody knew for sure whether these threats were real or merely tactical ploys to slow down the challenger, but my security people weren't taking any chances. They forced me to travel in different vehicles, constantly changing their routes and taking a series of other precautions. I was not scared. They could shoot me, and I knew Milosevic was ready to do it. All these thoughts would go through my mind—somebody shoots me, I become a fallen hero; Milosevic comes to the funeral, sheds a tear, and delivers a nice speech saying, "He was good American, and a good Serb, and he died for peace." That's what worried me. It seemed a nefarious plan, but also something that Milosevic and Vucelic could easily come up with.

Still, the Serbian people gave me courage. They had never seen a politician who joked with them, who wanted to hear about their problems, who talked about the virtue of compromise, and who insisted that their future was in their hands. They responded in kind. In my staff's view, the enthusiasm of the people was genuine. There was no doubt in their minds that I would be victorious—in a free and fair election. "I'd gone to enough political rallies," former senator Birch Bayh said. "I was convinced that the support for Milan was real. You could sense the enthusiasm. Whenever I saw that factory managers were going to keep him occupied for too long, I kept saying, 'Milan, you've got to go out and see the workers.' And he would do it and they were so enthused."

No spring chicken to politics, Bayh also knew better than anyone the challenge that remained. Even though every survey showed me in the lead, when Schoen asked voters who they thought would actually win the election, a four to one majority picked Milosevic. It was the only race that he was winning—the expectations game. Schoen tried to overcome the credibility gap by publicizing the results of his surveys, which showed me well ahead. His hope was that people would realize it was possible for me to win. "At moments of rationality and lucidity," Calef said later, "we could see Milosevic wasn't going to let this happen, but we still kept going. We latched onto this glimmer of hope that we'd be able to prevail."

The campaign was buoyed in mid-December by a long-sought endorsement. For weeks, Cosic had been wavering, seemingly playing both sides of the political fence. But on December 14, Cosic attacked his former protégé Milosevic directly, strongly backed my candidacy, and urged his countrymen to do the same.

Getting the United States on board was another matter. Bayh, Press, Schoen, and I all attempted to convince President-elect Clinton to come out with a statement of support for "the forces of democracy." An endorsement by the president-elect would have been even more significant than one by the outgoing Bush administration.

My staff and I knew our best hope for victory would be for the United States to make a dramatic last-minute endorsement of Serbia's democratic opposition—if not my candidacy—backed by a promise to ease sanctions in case Milosevic was defeated. As such, my advisors were heartened by stories in American papers endorsing my candidacy. Syndicated columnist William Pfaff wrote that I had "struggled with great courage to make peace and restore justice in [my] native country." I had a chance to win, Pfaff concluded, since "there are a great many Serbs who think [Milosevic's war policy] has been a criminal enterprise which will end in further horrors in Serbia itself."

Meanwhile, Bayh and Scanlan met with Madeleine Albright, then Clinton's foreign policy advisor. They made the same argument that I had outlined in a message to Eagleburger earlier in December: "If the ruling regime in Serbia is reelected, its policies are highly unlikely to change, and the United States is going to come under increasing domestic and foreign pressure to join in a very hazardous military intervention." But Albright offered no encouragement. Bill Press said later that Clinton was "too new, too green, and he did not want to take chances. Clinton wouldn't do it even though he liked Milan."

In a last-ditch effort, Scanlan and Rakic went separately to lobby Eagleburger. Rakic appealed to the secretary personally. He explained my desperate need for U.S. assistance. Any token gesture would do, as long as it sent a signal to the people of Serbia. Eagleburger's response was unchanging. "We can't do it," he told his old friend.

Scanlan, whose friendship with Eagleburger was long past repair, made a formal request. Four days before the end of the election campaign, he drove to Hungary, checked into the Budapest Hyatt, and phoned Eagleburger's assistant Bill Montgomery. With the presidential elections over, Jack said, the administration was no longer burdened by political considerations. "What we need is some sort of a statement," he told Montgomery. "Larry doesn't have to mention Panic by name, if he doesn't feel like it. We need something to the effect that if the Yugoslav people show the wisdom of opting for someone who is going to bring true democracy, then it will improve relations." Montgomery was guarded but indicated that something was in the works. "We think we can get something done," he told Scanlan. Recalling the conversation later, Montgomery insisted, however, that "we had a real question whether Panic would ever make any difference. Maybe we were wrong, but that was the way we thought at the time."

The day after Scanlan and Montgomery spoke, Eagleburger was due to leave for Geneva to attend yet another conference on the situation in the former Yugoslavia. There, we were once again disappointed. While issuing rhetorical platitudes that urged Serbia to "vote for peace" and "change," Eagleburger denounced Serbia and declared Milosevic and other key Bosnian Serb leaders as "war criminals" who were guilty of "crimes against humanity" for their actions in Bosnia. It's hard to imagine anything Eagleburger could have done that would be more detrimental to my electoral hopes. His remarks, which ignored me and inflamed the virus of Serbian nationalism, seemed almost designed to ensure my defeat and a Milosevic victory. From Milosevic's perspective, it also made an election victory that much more important. Defeated at the polls, his next stop might be The Hague and a war crimes tribunal.

Not surprisingly Eagleburger's statement created an extraordinary uproar in Serbia. Nationalists and former Communists seized on the speech as proof of America's animosity toward the Serbian people. Eagleburger's Geneva speech provided Milosevic with a unique opportunity, on the eve of a critical national election, to resuscitate his nationalist base and hint of an international conspiracy against the Serbian people. This was, Belgrade television declared in shrill tones, yet another in the familiar pattern of great power demands. Milosevic went first to Kosovo and then later to Nis with *New York Times* reporter John Burns to relay his response. In the newspaper's December 22, 1992, issue, Burns reported him declaring in martial tones, "This country has at many times in its history endured the challenge of foreign threats. . . . Now we are called upon once again to decide whether we will stand up, or go down on our knees and become a new Balkan colony. So I tell you: We will never surrender Serbia."

I was deeply shaken by Eagleburger's foolish words, since the American had long experience in Yugoslavia and supposedly knew Serbs. Over the years, I would debate time and again with myself whether Eagleburger knew what he was doing. David Owen once offered a curious insight about Eagleburger's intentions. "He did it, I think, to sort of justify his place in history," Owen argued. "It was sort of quixotic, you know. With everybody else being moralistic he wanted to put himself in the clear. Why not be the man who branded Slobodan Milosevic?" Publicly, however, Owen immediately put a distance between himself and Eagleburger by telling journalists that it is "difficult" to grasp Eagleburger's motives. "Why call someone a war criminal and then negotiate with him?" I often wondered the same thing.

There were further signs of the West's abdication of responsibility in Yugoslavia. When I asked a number of foreign groups for international observers to monitor the elections, the U.S. Helsinki Commission, an independent agency created by Congress to monitor compliance with a 1975 multination accord on European security and cooperation, agreed. But they then sent fewer than one hundred observers to monitor thousands of polling stations. In the final, tumultuous days of the campaign, meanwhile, Milosevic's campaign stressed Serbia's isolation and portrayed their candidate as the only person in Yugoslavia capable of standing up to the West.

With equal doses of anti-me and anti-American rhetoric, as well as free airtime on national television, Milosevic's message was the one that millions of Serbs saw on their televisions. Milosevic's final campaign speech was a masterpiece of nationalist invective, fully personifying Serbia's national cult of victimization. Before a crowd of thousands of party apparatchiks, Milosevic vowed that Serbia would never be brought to her knees by foreign powers. On the streets, Milosevic supporters wrote "U.S.A." across my face on campaign posters. Milosevic also resorted to old-fashioned political bribery. Taxes on farmers were postponed. Late fees on phone bills were wiped out. Pensions and state factory salaries were paid on time.

All the while, I struggled on. More than 150,000 people, many carrying lighted candles, attended my final rally in front of the parliament building on a balmy December evening. Milosevic, I thundered, was "the force of darkness" which had led Serbia into a catastrophe. "Milosevic wants to build a Great Wall of China around Serbia and have people live on the margins of poverty. Milosevic's Serbia is an outcast, isolated, humiliated, and wounded by sanctions." I noted that Milosevic's regime was one of "extremism that is portrayed as patriotism." "My quest is not a struggle for power," I told the crowd. "This is a struggle to change this system. That is the sole reason for my candidacy." I even told the assembled that, if elected, I would propose constitutional changes that would eliminate the position of Serbian president altogether. But few people outside Belgrade heard my speech. Radio Television Belgrade made only a passing reference to our huge rally, while

devoting almost four full hours of prime time to Milosevic's final campaign extravaganza.

On December 19, the day before the election, more disturbing news
came from the West. In Washington, the outgoing president Bush and
British prime minister John Major met and agreed on a new set of
measures against Serbia: tougher sanctions, including a complete break
in postal and telecommunication links, the freezing of all bank accounts
abroad held by Serbian citizens, and the sealing off of Serbia's borders.
But even with this additional fuel for Milosevic's campaign of grievance,
the desire for change remained strong. The polls showed a neck and
neck race. In Belgrade alone, more than 80 percent of the voters said
they would cast a ballot for me, and my aides were confident that I
would either win on the first ballot or the few minor candidates would
attract enough votes to force a runoff election. I hoped so.

Election Day, December 20, 1992—also my sixty-third birthday—
was unseasonably warm and sunny. Voter turnout was heavy, yet thousands were turned away. In Kosovo, the Albanians were true to their
word and boycotted the election. In an ominous sign of the troubles to
come, numerous instances of fraud and intimidation were reported
across the country. The worst fears of electoral manipulations were
quickly being realized. Election authorities had quietly purged from the
rolls all voters who had not participated in voting the previous spring.
Since the opposition parties had boycotted that election, cumbersome
and time-consuming procedures had been put in place for those who
wanted to be reinstated. The Helsinki Commission later estimated that
5 percent of eligible voters were not able to cast ballots because their
names were not found on voting lists.

The trickery did not end there. Many university students, who
strongly supported me, were required to register for subsidized housing
and pick up stipends for the next semester at their universities on election day. As such, many of them were not able to return to their home-
towns and villages to vote. Border crossings were practically shut down
to prevent Serbs and members of ethnic minorities working abroad to
vote. Even so, Schoen's exit polls showed Milosevic and me tied at 47
percent. In Belgrade, between 80 and 90 percent of those polled had
voted for me.

As my supporters gathered at my villa that evening, the crowd remained optimistic. A band was playing. People were dancing and having

a good time. Always the optimist, I moved from one group to another with banter and warm greetings. "We had a guy with a radio phone reporting results from Belgrade precincts," Calef recalled. "The first ten precincts went for Milan—overwhelmingly! Everybody cheered." But the jubilation was short-lived. The next set of results showed Milosevic far ahead. "When I saw that in one Belgrade precinct—Zemun—Panic received zero votes," Calef remembered, "I knew the election was rigged." According to Ted Olic, who closely monitored these developments, "The party machinery was defending itself. They invented a new route for ballots—they were sent from precincts to newly created county electoral boards instead of the Central Election Board, which was mandated by law." In other words, the Milosevic people had inserted an additional counting and checking process between the local and the federal level, and there they simply swapped boxes. Foreign observers estimated that roughly 10 to 15 percent of the ballot was rigged; our campaign believed the percentage was much higher.

Yet, even then, there was still hope. If the Helsinki Commission observers were in place to supervise the vote counting, there was still an opportunity to highlight the examples of vote theft and possibly annul the election results. But in a fitting coda to the West's continued indifference toward us, the observers left Belgrade on December 23—they wanted to go home for Christmas. As a result, no one was watching the vote count and the Milosevic forces could operate with virtual impunity. The next day, Christmas Eve, the central election commission declared Slobodan Milosevic the winner. In the end, with a 69 percent voter turnout, Milosevic garnered 56 percent of the vote; I had 34 percent.

After the damage had been done, a report by the Helsinki Commission declared that the elections were "neither free nor fair." "All international experts who observed the election campaign," it stated, "came to the conclusion that the governing party's complete control of nationwide electronic media—and its abuse of this power—made a fair campaign impossible. On election day, virtually every delegation that visited polling sites in Serbia witnessed irregularities in electoral administration, especially in voter registration; these irregularities disproportionately favored the governing party."

As the full scope of the fraud and intimidation became apparent, Deputy Prime Minister Ljubisa Rakic proposed that the election immediately be annulled by President Cosic and followed up by a declaration of martial law. The next morning Rakic drove to Cosic's house and urged him to do just that. "It's too late," Cosic shrugged. By this point, I was physically and emotionally drained and felt stung by the complete lack of Western support, and I saw little chance of success regardless.

Even as I felt reluctance, Milosevic's allies moved with a newfound brazenness. Within hours, Vojislav Seselj of the Radical Party publicly demanded my arrest. Interior Minister Bulatovic also warned the Americans that "Milosevic had phoned me and suggested that Panic be arrested and tried for treason." Seemingly, any trumped-up charge would do. According to Cosic, Milosevic informed him that he would have the police pick me up, but the Yugoslav president warned him against such a move. "I will not permit it," he told Milosevic, and the dictator backed down.

As the mood darkened in Belgrade, I urged all the American citizens on my staff to leave the country as soon and as quietly as possible. "The situation is dangerous and you have to leave," I told them. As Calef put it, "The reality dimension was setting in." The most vulnerable were American Serbs who were born in Yugoslavia, and who could be arrested as Yugoslav citizens. I spent a quiet Christmas with my wife Sally and longtime assistant Marcia O'Hagan. The women left the next day. Dejected, I escorted them to the plane.

On that same day, the U.S. embassy in Belgrade delivered to Milosevic a letter from President Bush. The Christmas letter, as it became known, outlined a new U.S. policy toward Kosovo: "In the event of a conflict caused by Serbian action, the United States will be prepared to employ military force against the Serbians in Kosovo and in Serbia proper." The irony of this was not lost on me—had the United States only supported my political effort, the threat of force would have likely been unnecessary. On December 29, with Milosevic now firmly in the driver's seat, the country's parliament adopted a no-confidence motion against my government. I was to remain the head of a caretaker administration until my successor could be named. "Take a vacation," Rakic urged me. "Go to California."

The next day, as I was preparing to make last-minute calls before returning home, I asked an aide to instruct the driver that I would be leaving in fifteen minutes. "Mr. Panic, the chauffeur is not here, nor is the car," I was told. "Nobody checked in this morning." I looked out the window from my residence—my official Mercedes 600 was not there.

Almost simultaneously, Milosevic removed the entire Yugoslav military leadership—the chief of staff and forty-four other top generals. All were sent into retirement.

On the last hour of the last day of 1992, I left Belgrade in a government plane bound for Copenhagen—I was the only passenger on board. "I'm never coming back," I muttered to myself as I was boarding the craft, "I'm never coming back." I felt an intense feeling of bitterness and failure. I had returned to Yugoslavia to save my native land from the scourges of nationalism and war. Now, despite all of my best efforts, it seemed that things were actually worse than when I had arrived months earlier. As Belgrade and Serbia receded into the darkness behind me, I confess my innate sense of optimism broke down. "What had it all been worth?" I mused. The answer did not come that night, and I ushered in 1993, angry and alone, some 30,000 feet above Germany.

10

COMING TO TERMS

In fact, I did return, and not long thereafter. After three weeks away from Serbia, I prepared to go back to Belgrade and wind up my affairs. In the meantime, Cosic had named me a "roving ambassador for peace." The *Wall Street Journal* had praised me as one of the "Europeans of the Year" for my "bold" campaign against Milosevic and success in being able to "galvanize Serbia's weak and scattered opposition." Not surprisingly, Milosevic wasn't impressed by these accolades. Rumors of my arrest and imprisonment floated in the air. Milosevic was going to take every opportunity to offer a final humiliation.

As my staff and I sought to reenter the country, we were detained by the Yugoslav police at the Hungarian border. At one point, a shootout between police and my security guards was only averted at the last moment as cooler heads prevailed. I was held for five hours at the police station before President Cosic managed to reach Milosevic. Cosic demanded to know if I had been arrested. "He has not been arrested yet," Milosevic said, "but we will arrest him and have his head and then you can pardon him!" "For God's sake, what's the matter with you!" cried Cosic. To Cosic, this was another of Milosevic's psychological games. He wanted to exhibit his power by toying with his enemies and savoring my humiliation. Cosic vigorously objected until the dictator relented.

Now prime minister only in name, I met with a group of Western journalists for dinner one evening in February 1993. I tried to conceal my anguish under a mask of courtesy and composure, but I felt a deep sadness when I talked of my experiences in Balkan politics—the missed opportunities, the lack of support from abroad, and the failures of will. Still, I refused to succumb completely to bitterness. It is not my way to look backward, or to waste energy in whining.

When studying for my citizenship exam years before, I had read about Abraham Lincoln, and one sentence remained stuck in my mind. In 1858, Lincoln unsuccessfully campaigned for the Senate against Stephen Douglas of Illinois. The main issue, of course, was slavery—Lincoln abhorred the institution and opposed its expansion into the West, while Douglas thought states should be able to decide for themselves if they wanted to allow the "peculiar institution" in their borders. Over the course of several historic debates, Lincoln laid out their differing perspectives in a simple and straightforward manner. "It is the eternal struggle," he once said, "between two principles—right and wrong— throughout the world." I took solace in the sense that I too had fought for the right thing, even in defeat. I felt sorry for the Serbs, sorry that I didn't accomplish more for them. But I am glad I tried, and that I planted a few seeds of change. The ancient Greeks used to say that happiness is full use of your powers while aiming at excellence. I struggled, and, even though the full use of my powers resulted in failure, I received more in return than I ever dreamed of.

Just before Radoje Kontic was named as my successor in late February 1993, I wrote an article for the London weekly *The European*. It was my parting shot against Milosevic and it laid out my vision for the future: "My term of office as prime minister of Yugoslavia will soon end. Thereafter, I intend to devote myself to supporting the development of democratic movements and processes in Yugoslavia, including the free and open informational infrastructure essential to the democratic process. Even more essential, in my view, is a populace assured of a much brighter economic future for themselves and their children. This can only come through regional economic cooperation. If your opportunities for security, the enjoyment of life, and the realization of your dreams are as good as your neighbor's, you are less likely to give in to the destructive nationalistic demagoguery of unscrupulous authoritarian politicians." I didn't have to elaborate on who I was talking about.

Contrary to what diplomats like Eagleburger had argued in the past, this initiative for change must come from the outside, I wrote. Europe first and foremost, with the support of the United States, should help stem the tide of regional economic collapse. I also envisioned a regional grouping named the Balkan Commonwealth of Independent States "enjoying peace and prosperity via regional tolerance and cooperation by the year 2000."

A year or so later, I could start to crack jokes about my political experience; the meetings with foreign leaders, the motorcycle escorts, even the security protection. "I'm one of the three Californians who have addressed the General Assembly of the United Nations," I would say to people who asked me of my time as prime minister. "The other two were Richard Nixon and Ronald Reagan." And with the benefit of hindsight, I was eventually able to talk about this experience with a considerable feeling of detachment.

But this took time, even for someone as optimistic as I am. In the immediate weeks after I returned to California, I was disillusioned and depressed, tired and sometimes bitter. I felt publicly humiliated, having been forced to flee Serbia—robbed of victory by Milosevic's massive and unpunished vote fraud. Now I was nothing more than a California businessman.

And I was not just angry at myself. More and more, I felt a growing sense of betrayal, particularly by the American and European leaders who had consistently undermined me. I thought of them as men in expensive suits with the power to stop the war—but who lacked even a fundamental understanding of conflict in the Balkans. The ghosts of the past can and should be conquered. This was not some age-old animosity inexorably unfolding in the former Yugoslavia—the bloodshed and deprivation there were being manifested by cynical political leaders, more than happy to twist nationalism and ethnicity for their own purposes. During the election campaign, I had seen and felt firsthand the Serbian people's overwhelming desire for change. The solution was simple, even if the West could not see it: Remove the cynical leaders from power, make the case for peace, and peace would follow.

What I advocated was seemingly too simple, too obvious and clear-headed to be acceptable to the intellectuals and foreign policy gurus. I had argued for reconciliation, a Marshall Plan for the region, and a commitment to take on the Balkans' real enemies—ignorance, poverty, despotism, and aggressive nationalism. But in the European Union and the United States, there was a genuine mismatch between political rhetoric and political will. Few countries were willing to spend the necessary money or exercise genuine political capital on behalf of peace. The European Union was hamstrung by its inability to marry the very real and separate interests of its disparate members. And while the United States had the political, military, and economic resources to make a difference, Washington refused to get engaged.

I was always amazed by this shortsightedness. For a fraction of the same amount spent on military deployments in the Balkans, the United States could have given my campaign the support it needed to unseat Milosevic—with quite a bit left over for economic reconstruction. And who knows how differently Balkan history might have unfolded?

Tragically for the Serbian people, that was not to be. If anything, the new Democratic administration—and the new U.S. president—turned out to be as fatalistic as its predecessor about the region. Clinton, who was relatively unversed in foreign policy, read Robert Kaplan's *Balkan Ghosts* and seemed to share the writer's gloomy view that violence in the Balkans was unavoidable. In Clinton's mind, as in Eagleburger's before him, only when the Serbs, Croats, and Muslims got tired of killing each other would the war ever end. In Washington, D.C., a city uncommonly susceptible to groupthink, this became the bipartisan conventional wisdom.

Even more galling to me was the growing anti-Serb veneer of both American policy and subsequent media coverage in the region. I wasn't completely naïve. I understood that the Serbs were committing the lion's share of terrible crimes in Bosnia. Yet, at the same time, as prime minister I had seen firsthand accounts of horrific Muslim massacres of both Serb and Croat civilians. To facilitate making a morality play out of the Balkan crisis, the international community seemed to ignore what little they heard of these atrocities.

These frustrations would only continue. In the spring of 1993, Vance and Owen of the UN and EU unveiled their plan for peace. I, among others, had worked closely with the two men in putting together their proposal. While imperfect and largely a stopgap measure, the plan offered a commonsense approach for ending the violence. It called for a division of Bosnia into ten cantons—three with a Serb majority, two with a Croat majority, three with a Muslim majority, and one mixed Muslim-Croat. Sarajevo, the capital, was the tenth canton, patterned after the District of Columbia, with all three ethnic groups sharing power and accorded the same influence and privileges.

Not surprisingly, Karadzic opposed the plan, as the Bosnian Serbs would be forced to give up 20 percent of their conquered territory. Many Bosnian Muslims were also adamantly opposed, because it undermined the notion of Bosnia as a multiethnic state. Milosevic, who was increasingly trying to repair his international image, went along and put extraordinary pressure on Karadzic to go along with the agreement. But here again, the United States refused to support a plan for peace. The Clinton administration argued that it would legitimize ethnic cleansing. From my perspective, the United States was standing on principle at the cost of potentially thousands more civilian casualties. Moreover, the whole idea that it endorsed ethnic cleansing was based largely on an incorrect reading of the true nature of the conflict—this was a civil war between three opposed groups who, outside of Sarajevo, generally lived in separate communities. In fact, the major reason that the United States opposed the plan was that it would have required the president to send thousands of soldiers to the region in order to keep the peace.

I offered my expertise and assistance to Clinton, but was referred to Leon Fuerth, Vice President Gore's foreign policy advisor, and Madeleine Albright, the U.S. ambassador to the United Nations. After only a few minutes with the downright-unfriendly Fuerth, who dismissed the Vance-Owen plan out of hand, I realized I was talking to a brick wall. I then went to New York to meet with Albright. Albright was more congenial than Fuerth, but similarly dismissive of the Vance-Owen plan. In fact, Vance and Owen themselves attended this meeting and left visibly upset. Vance, normally calm and composed, could not conceal his anger. His lower lip started trembling so much that I was afraid he would have a heart attack. By the time our meeting was over, I knew that the Vance-Owen plan was dead in the water, at least as far as the new administration was concerned.

In April, Secretary of State Warren Christopher traveled to Europe soliciting support for an American plan that would entail lifting the arms embargo on Bosnia, while at the same time bombing Bosnian Serb positions. This was the so-called "lift and strike" plan. But the Europeans who still had peacekeepers on the ground were in no way interested in putting their troops in harm's way.

And so the violence continued, and my feelings of frustration grew more palpable. My wife Sally says I was being increasingly temperamental, edgy, and deeply sensitive to even the smallest slight. This was a very painful period for me, but I would ultimately characterize it as an enriching experience that I learned from. Sally thinks the frustration would have sent me to an early grave, if not for a sudden separate struggle—one that would embroil me in a battle to keep control of ICN.

While I was in Yugoslavia, a flamboyant Beverly Hills broker named Rafi Khan had begun a sustained campaign of buying up ICN stock for his institutional clients. Khan had at one time seemed a strong supporter of ICN, and of me in particular. When the company had proposed a new stock offering for Viratek, a publicly traded subsidiary of ICN, Khan helped organize the road show to spark investor interest. But unbeknownst to me or ICN, Khan was in fact using the opportunity to talk to various brokerage houses about a possible takeover of the company. In the spring of 1993, alleging that I was overpaid and ICN poorly managed, Khan assembled a large group of institutional investors who were prepared to back him in his takeover effort.

The odds in this fight were not in my favor. The cumulative effect of SEC investigations and FDA foot-dragging on ribavirin, as well as my sojourn in Balkan politics and a declining stock price, risked stacking the deck against me. To many, the situation seemed hopeless. "Frankly, the odds were so much against him that I couldn't see how he could get through it," recalls my son-in-law, Mark. But I felt as if someone was trying to take away my baby, and this proxy battle eclipsed all my other concerns. I threw myself back into my old job, conducting round-the-clock strategy sessions with Adam Jerney, Roberts Smith, and other top aides, as well as with lawyers in California and New York.

As it happened, this corporate battle was a blessing in disguise. I have always been at my happiest and most vigorous when on the job. And, with no time to wallow in the frustration of my Balkan experience, I felt revitalized by this uphill struggle to save my company. Each morning, I was at my Costa Mesa office by 6:30 a.m. After everyone had long gone, I was still at my desk, working the phones and trying to persuade larger institutional investors to support my management. My lawyers also sued Khan in federal court in New York. That move was considered unlikely to succeed, but it proved to be Khan's undoing and provided me with the lifeline I needed.

"We knew all along that Khan was a shady character," my lawyer Clifford Saffron recalled. "But we pulled a rabbit out of the hat. We took out a full page ad in the *Wall Street Journal*. It read, 'DON'T BE CONNED BY KHAN.' The next day we got a call from Khan's cousin who lived in Milwaukee. He said Khan was wanted for fraud in England where an arrest warrant had been issued." Saffron immediately phoned Scotland Yard, which confirmed that Khan indeed was wanted for questioning in connection with a stock scam. Saffron took the next plane for London to meet with Scotland Yard inspector Jackie Malton, who was in charge of the investigation. Malton agreed to fly to New York to testify in court the next day.

The appearance of a Scotland Yard inspector provided another bizarre twist to the unfolding drama in Judge John Sprizzo's courtroom. "The judge loved it," Saffron recalled. Malton's testimony made clear that Khan had failed to disclose material information in his SEC filings. That was enough. The judge accused Khan of committing perjury and described several of the individuals who testified on his behalf as creatures out of the underworld.

Not surprisingly, the revelations fatally undermined Khan's credibility with many of the institutional investors who pledged to support his takeover bid. While clearly ICN and I had some housecleaning to do, few investors were prepared to turn over the company to a shady operator like Khan. On February 2, 1994, over 90 percent of the voting shares rejected Khan's proposal to replace me and the board of directors.

My battle with Rafi Khan ended in a surprising victory, and I very much needed one at that moment. Once it was over, however, I again dived back into the maelstrom of the Balkans. Like everything in my life, once I sunk my teeth into something I could never let it go. Even at a time when war was continuing to rage in Bosnia, I traveled across Europe, meeting with national leaders and trying to build support for efforts at economic cooperation in the region. "Billions of dollars are being spent on peacekeeping forces that have been unable to keep the peace," I argued in a January 1994 piece in the *European*. "Additional billions are being spent on humanitarian assistance . . . surely an international program of assistance to promote regional economic cooperation that would lay the foundation for lasting peace and stability in the Balkans would be money better spent."

I strongly believed that, if the Yugoslavs were ever to move beyond the slights of the past, they would need proper "incentive" and the "prospect of a better future" in order to do so. Ever since my days as a poor immigrant in California, my faith in the redemptive power of economic opportunity has never wavered. As I once put it in a speech at the University of Central Europe in Budapest, "What is life all about when you move beyond the basic issues of survival and security? Simply the desire to create the basis for a better life for your children and grandchildren."

Back in Belgrade, and still looking to improve ties with the new U.S. president, Slobodan Milosevic had begun sharply scaling down his anti-American rhetoric. Serbia was suffocating under UN sanctions, regressing into destitution as inflation soared to astronomical levels. Milosevic wanted to derail a new package of restrictive financial measures being discussed in the United Nations Security Council. In May 1993, he had severed his links with the Bosnian Serb leaders when they refused to endorse the Vance-Owen Peace Plan. Long dismissive in private of the "Bosnian knuckleheads," Milosevic was more than happy to cut off aid to them and close the border with Bosnia. As a result, he was slowly and improbably beginning to establish himself in the eyes of the international community as a peacemaker capable of making serious concessions, perhaps even the key to peace in the Balkans.

While Milosevic gained respect overseas, he took the opportunity to settle domestic scores with his last remaining potential rivals. In the same month he broke with Karadzic, he at last engineered the dismissal of Dobrica Cosic as Yugoslavian president. (Milosevic didn't bother to tell him in person—Cosic's wife heard the news on the radio.) Soon after, the police moved against Milosevic's main opposition opponent, Vuk Draskovic, and his wife. Draskovic was a former nationalist who had become concerned with the direction of Serbian nationalism and who was dismayed by Milosevic's increasingly autocratic style. A charismatic man and the nation's leading opposition figure, he was both loathed and feared by Milosevic.

Shortly after Cosic was removed, Draskovic spoke at an antigovernment demonstration near the parliament building. After he left, scuffles broke out and a Serb policeman was seriously wounded. The opportunity arose for Milosevic to finally deal with his hated rival for good. Police arrived at Draskovic's party headquarters late in the evening to arrest the opposition leader. He and his wife were savagely beaten, revived, and then pummeled again as they ran a police gauntlet. As they lay bloodied in the street, police officers screamed at Draskovic's wife, "We have been waiting for you, you whore." Soon, more blows rained down up on them.

Draskovic's head injuries were so grave that prison authorities were forced to move him to a neurological clinic for observation. Convinced he was going to die in prison, Draskovic began a hunger strike to force his release. After furious international outcry and mass demonstrations, Draskovic was released. But the point was made: If the main opposition leader could be treated this way before the whole world, what could other opponents of the regime expect? The subsequent period saw a growing alienation of the educated classes and a further consolidation of the dictator's power.

Bill Clinton condemned the arrest of Draskovic, but Milosevic's atrocious behavior didn't stop international diplomats from continuing to talk with him. Indeed, it was as if nothing had happened. Instead, Lord Owen talked about fresh hopes for a quick end to the Bosnian war as a result of Milosevic's new policies there. I thought Owen's Milosevic-coddling approach was obviously wrong. "Milosevic is the problem, not the solution," I kept saying to anyone who would listen. But nobody was interested. The West, I concluded, was ready to let Milosevic off the hook if he would help end the Bosnian war—and keep their troops out of harm's way. How wrong was Owen again.

As I watched my native land plunge further into turmoil, Serbia once again became my overriding passion. When in Europe, I regularly stopped in Belgrade, kept in touch with opposition groups in Serbia, and visited provincial towns for talks with local leaders. Back at home, I continued to try to influence President Clinton.

I was convinced that a forceful diplomatic initiative by the United States could bring the Bosnian war to an end. I worked to persuade the president to follow the example of Jimmy Carter and get the belligerent parties together at the presidential retreat Camp David in order to hammer out a deal. I was also convinced that only a modern and multi-ethnic Bosnia—not divided ethnic enclaves—would have a chance at survival and genuine economic growth. And the United States could be an effective mediator only if it adopted an evenhanded position toward all parties.

In November 1994, I got a chance, with Birch Bayh and Jack Scanlan in tow, to meet with Clinton to discuss my ideas. I told the president that I had been in Belgrade the previous week and had discussed a possible Camp David-style meeting with several politicians, including Karadzic, who now accepted the proposed 51–49 percent division of land and the status of Sarajevo as an open city shared by the three ethnic communities. I was contemptuous of Karadzic's brutish and crude nationalism, but I also understood the Bosnian Serb leader needed political cover if he were to abandon the Serbs' significant territorial gains.

Karadzic, I told President Clinton, "needs to have some token of compromise in order to ensure that the agreement is supported by the Bosnian Serb population. The Serbian people need to hear from you that we in the United States do not hold them collectively responsible for the policies of their leaders." Clinton smiled, saying he fully understood the point. The most significant moment of a recent trip to the Middle East, he said, came during his speech to the Jordanian parliament. "We in the United States respect Islam," he had told the legislators. "It was like a bolt of lightning," Clinton said. "They did not expect this. And boy, did they applaud."

The moment was ripe, I implored, for a presidential initiative to end the Bosnian war. "I'm sure Milosevic would agree to something like this, but how could he deliver the Bosnian Serbs?" Clinton asked. Then there were the Bosnian Muslims and Croats. "How can I be sure they will come if I invite them?" "Mr. President, if you invite them to Camp David they will have to come," I replied. "Not Camp David," Clinton quipped and laughed. "It's too close to Washington."

Judging from Clinton's demeanor, I felt my arguments were having an impact. The one-on-one talk seemed to focus Clinton's mind on the problem far more than our exchange of letters. But political events soon forced Clinton to back off from a proactive approach. After Democrats lost control of the House and Senate in the 1994 midterm elections, he seemed considerably less inclined to embrace a major foreign policy initiative. Moreover, his advisors continued to favor the use of force as a means of punishing Bosnian Serbs, especially after it became evident they no longer enjoyed Milosevic's backing.

To help ensure that the Milosevic-Karadzic feud remained "irreversible," the United States rewarded Milosevic by lifting the three-year ban on Yugoslavia's participation in international sporting events. When I heard the news, I could only shake my head. How many times had I begged the United States for that same token of support? In any case, the move had little practical effect. The violence continued and, while Milosevic pledged to cut off support for his Serb brethren, it was clear that somehow they were still getting assistance.

In March 1995, I again wrote to Clinton and urged him to call for a summit meeting on Bosnia. My letter provided a piece of intelligence: Many political sources in Belgrade, I said, "suspect that Milosevic would abandon the Bosnian and Krajina Serbs if necessary to preserve his own political position." Clinton's reply was terse: "We will keep your suggestion for a high-level conference in mind," the president replied, "but continue to believe it would be a premature move at this time." But, premature or no, events on the ground would soon fundamentally alter the political dynamic in the Balkans, and force the West to finally act.

11

A TURNING POINT

In June 1995, NATO planes mounted what was billed as a sustained bombing campaign against the Bosnian Serbs, hitting strategic targets and blowing up two large ammunition depots in eastern Bosnia. Karadzic retaliated by seizing UN peacekeepers as hostages. A total of 375 British, French, and Canadian soldiers were chained to potential bombing targets in the mountains of Bosnia. This grim sight was shown both on Bosnian Serb television and televisions throughout the world. Soon after, the air strikes stopped. And then Milosevic stepped in. After weeks of negotiations, he secured the release of the peacekeepers. He began to look like a genuine convert to peacemaking. In fact, I had prevailed upon Milosevic's aide, Mitevic, to convince the dictator to do the right thing for the Serbian people.

Western governments now felt indebted to Milosevic, but both the British and the French, who had provided the bulk of the peacekeeping troops during the seemingly endless conflict, were now ready to wash their hands of Bosnia. Shortly after their hostages were released, the British and French governments quietly informed Washington that they planned to withdraw their forces from Bosnia in the fall. Now, it seemed, there was a distinct prospect that the UN peacekeeping operation in Bosnia would simply collapse. This put President Clinton in a bind: Not only would it practically embolden a full-scale Serb assault, it would force the president to uphold his prior pledge to commit twenty thousand U.S. troops to help the allies extricate their troops from Bosnia. The worst possible scenario seemed the only option—deploying

American combat troops on a risky mission in the midst of an ethnic war.

Still working the president's ear, I kept urging Clinton to seek a negotiated solution and repeatedly asked him to address the Serb nation directly: "Serbs have long waited in vain to hear that they are not held collectively responsible for the policies of Milosevic," I insisted. I strongly believed a Western ultimatum to the Bosnian Serbs would be counterproductive, and tried to explain the character of the people who have the reputation of being the most pugnaciously stubborn of all the Yugoslavs. The Bosnian Serbs were ready to resume talks, I told Clinton, if not presented with a take it or leave it ultimatum. Clinton disputed the last point. The hostage taking and the Bosnian Serb offensives in Eastern Bosnia "do not reflect their claims of being prepared to resume peace negotiations," he replied.

While Clinton was still searching for options, the Bosnian Serbs next moved to seize Muslim enclaves that had been declared "safe areas" under UN protection. Guarded by meager UN forces with restrictive rules of engagement, they were ripe for Serbian picking. For the Serbs, the most irritating of these was the city of Srebrenica. A local center for silver mining only a short distance from the Serbian border, Srebrenica was then serving as a (presumably) safe haven for thousands of Muslim refugees. However, it was also being used by Bosnian Muslims as a base from which to launch hit-and-run attacks against the Serbs. In January 1993, one such attack occurred in Visnice, the home village of Ratko Mladic, a Bosnian Serb army commander. Houses were burned to the ground and some of the Serb victims were beheaded, their heads lined up along the roadside—a practice introduced by Afghan and Arab mujahideen who served in the Muslim forces.

On July 12, 1995, a Bosnian Serb unit under Mladic's command, along with a paramilitary unit from Serbia, attacked Srebrenica; brushed aside the UN peacekeepers; and, in a few hours, overran the Muslim defense. The Muslims begged Dutch UN peacekeepers for help, but Mladic told the Dutch commander, "I'm in charge here. I'll decide what happens." In a television interview, he declared that no one would be harmed and that the refugees would be evacuated. They had "nothing to fear," he claimed—but they did. In what is today known as the Srebrenica massacre—the largest mass murder in Europe since World War II—over eight thousand men and boys, as well as dozens of women and girls, were killed, and many other women and young girls were raped.

When news of the atrocity reached Western capitals, any remaining reticence about getting involved in the Bosnian conflict quickly disappeared. Western anger was only heightened by the extraordinary feelings of guilt. Under the mandate of the United Nations, the Western allies had pledged to protect Bosnia's Muslim safe havens—clearly, they had failed in that mission. I myself was appalled by the acts. They filled me with a powerful sense of self-hatred. How could my own people commit such heinous acts? How could Serbs act with such utter inhumanity? Whatever might have happened in the past, there could be no defense for the Serbian atrocities in Srebrenica. The Serbs now had to face up to the crimes they had committed in the name of nationalism.

As for the peace process, I believed that the events in Srebrenica represented a genuine step backward—they only served to reaffirm the notion in the West that all evil had been perpetrated by Serbs, and that the Muslims and Croats were blameless. Indeed, after Srebrenica, it was practically impossible for any Serb to argue otherwise. And yet, most bothersome of all, the man who had launched the mayhem and violence in Bosnia—Slobodan Milosevic—had now become the West's principal hope for Balkan peace. Without Milosevic's support for aggressive Serbian nationalism and material assistance to the Bosnian Serbs, Srebrenica would likely never have happened. I found it all infuriating.

Clinton was also outraged by the event—not simply for the wanton atrocity, but for the extent to which it dramatized the West's passivity in the face of Serb aggression. Not only had the UN peacekeepers in Srebrenica done nothing to stop the violence, the indecision of the United States and its European allies had seemingly emboldened the Bosnian Serbs to believe their actions would face no consequences. Determined to lift the Bosnian problem out of the slowly grinding machinery of government, Clinton appointed veteran diplomat Richard Holbrooke as his personal envoy, with full powers to settle the war. Unfortunately, this was probably the worst thing the president could have done.

Holbrooke was not a newcomer to the Balkans. In 1992, he had written a piece for *Newsweek* alerting the United States to the growing depravity taking place in the former Yugoslavia. Now, three years later, he brought a fresh perspective to the crisis. Moreover, he possessed a clear mandate from the American president, and a good relationship with Milosevic. Each man seemed to enjoy the other's rough sense of humor and brutal frankness. Unfortunately, both men were also richly cynical and knowingly used each other for political purposes. Milosevic "delivered" the Bosnian Serbs to Holbrooke. The American diplomat, in turn, helped Milosevic reinvent himself as a peacemaker.

Soon after Holbrooke's arrival, the Balkan calamity grew even more dire. On August 4, the Croatian president, Franjo Tudjman, decided to take care of the Serb minority in his country. Earlier in the year, he had expelled the UN peacekeepers serving as a buffer force between Croatian army troops and Croatian Serb forces in the Serb-dominated region of Krajina. Now, the Croatian troops—armed with the help of Iran and other Middle Eastern countries and trained by U.S. military advisors—quickly overran Serb military forces. With tacit American backing, they continued their offensive into Banja Luka, the largest Serb-held city in Bosnia. For the first time since the war began, the Bosnian Serbs found themselves on the defensive. Then, on August 28, Serb forces fired rockets into a market in the Muslim-populated city of Sarajevo, killing thirty-seven people. These were only a few of thousands fired by Bosnian Serb forces against Sarajevoans during the war, but this fusillade finally forced the hand of the West.

With cruise missiles and American bombers thrown into the fight, a massive display of NATO firepower was unleashed against the Bosnian Serbs. Milosevic had tacitly agreed to the bombing before it began—he wanted to both humiliate and punish the Bosnian Serb leaders and, at the same time, be relieved of any responsibility for their capitulation. But Tudjman wasn't simply interested in unifying his nation—he wanted to purify it. For centuries, Serbs had lived in the Krajina region of Croatia. In 1995 that would end. Some two hundred thousand Krajina Serbs were forced out of their homes. Those who stayed behind were killed and their homes torched. And yet, here the Western allies and international press corps largely remained silent. Carl Bildt, a former Swedish prime minister who had replaced David Owen as the EU's peace negotiator, was a notable exception. Shocked by the Croat brutality, he called on the Hague war crimes tribunal to investigate Tudjman on charges of "ethnic cleansing."

I protested vigorously to President Clinton, sending two letters within a week. The first denounced the Croats for a "callous disregard for the UN peacekeeping forces." The second expressed my outrage over the "ethnic cleansing undertaken with impunity" by the Croats. I added that America's criticism of such actions seemed to be "reserved exclusively for the Serbs." Clinton did not reply.

Few people expressed sympathy for the plight of "ethnically cleansed" Serb refugees, least of all Milosevic. His wife went so far as to publicly attack them. "Why didn't they defend their hearth?" she wrote in a newspaper column. "Why did they come here [to Serbia] at all?" Milosevic, the man who had fanned the flames of Serbian nationalism for years, didn't bother to visit or acknowledge the presence of the refugees. In 1992, they had been a convenient political weapon at his disposal. By 1995, they were simply another inconvenient problem.

In any case, Holbrooke now concluded that the road to a peace agreement was open. In late September, Clinton solicited my views on how to proceed with the peace negotiations. I reiterated my view that the president should invite the presidents of Serbia, Croatia, and Bosnia to Camp David. "When faced with your formal invitation, none of them could afford to hesitate or seek to impose conditions," I wrote him. Other key international players should also be invited as well, I thought, to convince the warring parties that they must make some hard decisions.

"I have been considering the idea of a Balkan peace conference along the lines proposed in your recent letter," Clinton replied on October 3. I hoped Holbrooke would officially present the proposal. A month later, on November 1, 1995, a peace conference opened at Wright-Patterson Air Force Base near Dayton, Ohio—the location was chosen to prevent the participants from negotiating in the press. Milosevic from Serbia, Tudjman from Croatia, and Izetbegovic from Bosnia sat down with Holbrooke, U.S. secretary of state Warren Christopher, and other officials, including General Wesley Clark. Clinton adopted the format I suggested, but the spirit of compromise was lacking—instead, this was old-fashioned arm-twisting. An agreement was pushed on the parties, with Milosevic, a man once branded a war criminal by Eagleburger, seemingly serving as the guarantor of America's diplomatic effort.

Behind the scenes, Milosevic had the temerity to seek out my advice, even during the negotiations. After all, I knew the Americans better than any of Milosevic's advisors. My message to him was clear: Do whatever the Americans say. "Your best course is to play the peacemaker card," I told Milosevic. Whenever stumbling blocks appeared, Milosevic should "act magnanimously." The dictator mostly followed my advice. For example, Muslims wanted the whole of Sarajevo, while Holbrooke's plan called for an open city modeled on Washington, D.C. At the crucial moment, when failure seemed inevitable, Milosevic gave Sarajevo to the Muslims as a "gift." Time after time, in fact, Milosevic made "concessions for peace" in the negotiations—mostly involving selling out the Bosnian Serbs who had outlived their political usefulness to him.

I hated that this conciliatory approach would further improve Milosevic's image in the West and make him seem more committed to peace than he ever in fact was. For years, I had warned Western negotiators that the diplomatic dance they consistently performed with Milosevic only added to the brutal dictator's legitimacy. Nevertheless, I also believed that, without an end to the fighting in Bosnia, there was no hope for the region. Stopping the killing and beginning the process of political and economic reconstruction had to come first.

In many respects, Dayton felt like a hollow victory. Milosevic, the architect of so much of the bloodshed and unrest in the Balkans, had succeeded in reinventing himself as a man of peace. I also knew that the "victory" would have a terribly demoralizing effect on Serbia's opposition. But I also understood that Dayton represented a unique opportunity to move forward. "The long-term viability and success of the [Dayton] peace agreement," I privately told Clinton, "will be determined by nonmilitary activities." As such, I urged the president to follow up with a comprehensive economic program, warning that piecemeal aid given to select countries "will increase rather than decrease tensions."

Shortly after Dayton, I addressed an economic conference in Washington on the former Yugoslavia. "Some foreign assistance must necessarily be targeted for reconstruction in the most heavily damaged areas of Bosnia and Croatia," I argued. But, above all else, "the programs and policies of the United States and the European Union should be designed to promote area-wide economic cooperation. This is why we need a Southeastern European Free Trade Association, [to] help lift the economic borders and ensure that funds are funneled directly to businesses and not through endless layers of government bureaucracy." Only by moving forward on economic reconstruction could the harmful effects of Milosevic's rule be ameliorated. But newfound respect from the West, I knew, would also further embolden Milosevic's dictatorial behavior—particularly toward Serbia's democratic opposition. Nonetheless, this heavy price was better than war.

By now, I had soured on the notion that America would help end the dictatorship in my homeland. More and more, I became convinced that Serbia must rid itself of Milosevic through its own efforts. So, while I continued cultivating links to Clinton and other American politicians, I also refocused my energy and efforts toward promoting democracy within Yugoslavia. By 1996, I had established myself as an unofficial ambassador for Yugoslavia's democratic opposition in the United States. I funded opposition groups and causes in Serbia and used Doug Schoen's expertise in polling to test the public mood of ordinary Serbians.

If anything, I felt more committed to the cause than ever: The events of the past four years—both the frustration of my own tenure as prime minister and my inability to persuade U.S. policy makers to come out against Milosevic—had convinced me that it was ultimately up to me. My mission in life became to bring peace and democracy to Serbia.

In fighting to help the Serbian opposition, my voice was an unusual one in American debates over Yugoslavia. Many American Serbs preferred to stay quiet, so as to avoid being viewed as Serb apologists. A few other wealthy Serb expatriates publicly protested against Washington's policy, but their financial contributions were modest at best. On one occasion, when I met well-off Serb expatriates whose names featured prominently in the Belgrade press, I tried to smoke them out. "Okay," I said, "let's raise money for Serbia right now. I'll go first: I'll donate one million in cash and another million in logistics and manpower through my firm." The other two demurred. "Milan," they said, "money isn't everything, but we'll lend our names to the cause." Names, I knew, were not going to get it done.

Meanwhile, pressures against Milosevic receded with the end of fighting in Bosnia. After Dayton, his public persona abroad was that of peacemaker and reborn democrat—it was as if his role in opening the floodgates of Balkan nationalism had never happened. I was particularly

troubled by Milosevic's new remaking, because I felt it shifted responsibility for his crimes onto all the Serbs. Still, Doug Schoen's public
opinion polls showed that Milosevic was supported by less than a third
of the Serb population. Since 1990, he and his party had only won
elections through systematic fraud—if the country ever had free and
fair elections, the dictator would not win. So I directed my energies
toward developing broad-based democratic institutions in Serbia, especially at the grassroots level. If given the opportunity of 1992 again, I
vowed to myself, this time I would not fail.

Initially I relied on my former government colleagues, but I also
stayed on good terms with former Milosevic supporters—including Dusan Mitevic, who had been witness to Milosevic's promise to step down
back in 1992. The main thrust of my effort was to get *all* of the regime
opponents—mild nationalists, progressive liberals, disillusioned socialists—to set aside their differences and form a united front. Above all, I
wanted to forge solid links with the rank-and-file opposition activists in
the provinces. This took up most of my time. "We went to Pancevo, Nis,
Novi Sad, other places, talking to local leaders," Rakic recalled. "We
talked to groups, up to one thousand people. The response was terrific."
I even discovered I had many admirers in the ruling Socialist Party. The
desire for change now stretched across all elements of Serbian society.

In the spring of 1996 in Nis, the main city in southern Serbia, I and
other opposition leaders formed a coalition to take on Milosevic, which
we called Savez za Promene—Alliance for Change. We were immediately attacked by the Milosevic government as representatives of, and
downright lackeys for, foreign interests. It was the usual line of attack
from Milosevic, fully intended to inflame nationalist passions and play
on the age-old notion of Serb victimization. But, this time, the attacks
also helped to publicize the alliance, which included most of the prominent opposition politicians.

One nonpolitician to join the group was Dragoslav Avramovic, an
economist who had spent most of his adult life in the United States,
with whom I had cultivated a close relationship. A diminutive man with
a warm smile, incisive mind, and a wide range of experience, Avramovic—biographically speaking—was well suited to play a leading role in
the post–Cold War Yugoslavia. Animated by a great passion and real
concern for the plight of emerging nations, he had joined the staff of
the World Bank in Washington in 1953, where he rose through the

ranks to become director of the development economics department. After retiring in 1978, he became director of the secretariat of the Brandt Commission on International Developmental Issues. Chaired by former German chancellor Willy Brandt, this commission had studied relations between the developed and developing worlds.

Over the years, Avramovic had become as concerned as I was about the fate of our native country. In 1993, he left his comfortable Rockville, Maryland, home and went to Belgrade to offer his services. Yugoslavia was in the deadly grip of an inflation that was ravaging the economy, and Milosevic asked him to take charge of the Yugoslav Central Bank. Already in his seventies, Avramovic succeeded spectacularly in bringing down inflation and stabilizing the economy. By 1994, he had gained great popularity—to many, he was affectionately known as Deda Avram, "Grandpa Avram." After Dayton, however, he was no longer needed by Milosevic. When he continued to insist on market-related economic reforms, Milosevic had enough and sent him back to the United States. As far as the dictator was concerned, Avramovic had now also exhausted his usefulness.

With my encouragement, Avramovic, then seventy-six, agreed to lead the coalition in the upcoming elections for the federal parliament and local councils. At the same time, I also wanted to encourage and support a new generation of Serbian politicians. One favorite was Zoran Djindjic, a German-educated academic with sparkling eyes and a boyish grin. As a student activist in the late 1960s, he was imprisoned by Tito's government. When released, he had decamped to Germany to complete his education and begin an academic career. When he returned to Belgrade in 1989, he became involved in politics. However, his Democratic Party was tiny, and, in a desperate search for nationalist support, Djindjic had strayed well away from his democratic roots, even supporting Karadzic and the Bosnian Serbs. To many Serbs he came across as a man without a clear vision, and his negative ratings were quite high.

Another important ally was Milo Djukanovic, prime minister of Montenegro and a key opponent of Milosevic. Still in his early thirties in the mid-1990s, Djukanovic, a shrewd bureaucratic operator who started his career as a Milosevic ally, was tall, handsome, smart, and opportunistic. Like Cosic and others, he had quickly realized that Serbia could not stand up to the world. Beginning in 1993, he began distancing himself both from the Bosnian war, which he regarded as a purely Serbian affair, as well as Milosevic, whom he privately considered a narrow-minded brute.

I saw Djukanovic as the country's most significant opposition figure. He was not a brand name like "Grandpa" Avramovic, but he was a formidable political presence who could limit Milosevic's maneuvering space. As prime minister of the tiny republic of Montenegro, the only (and much junior) partner of Serbia in what remained of Yugoslavia, he nonetheless had a true power base, not to mention a police force of fifteen thousand. For a number of months, Djukanovic and I were in almost daily telephone contact, discussing our political strategy. The plan was for Montenegro to push for greater autonomy from Serbia, but do so in such a way as to avoid provoking a military conflict. Meanwhile, I urged U.S. policy makers to actively support Djukanovic. I brought him to the United States and introduced him to President Clinton and other senior officials. The friendly U.S. reception emboldened Djukanovic, and he began offering material support to Serbia's opposition politicians and safe haven to those whose lives were in danger.

Besides political involvement, a personal matter also conspired to keep me in Yugoslavia for extended periods. I had met a talented, young star of the Belgrade Opera, Melena Kitic. For much of 1996 and 1997, we would keep our affair secret, but in 1998, I divorced Sally and married Melena. Three years later, she gave birth to a second Milan Jr, whom I dote on to this day.

Meanwhile, Milosevic continued to consolidate his power. The last remnants of an independent press—a daily newspaper, *Nasa Borba*, and a local television station, Studio B—were taken over by the regime. The Belgrade offices of the Soros Foundation, which had been helping finance many of the country's independent news sources, were also closed down. In all, 140 radio stations and 4 television stations were shuttered away. Lacking any access to the media now, alliance activists campaigned quietly during the summer and fall of 1996 in the towns and villages of Serbia, preparing for the September elections. With Milosevic's urging, the Yugoslav legislature moved to increase the number of electoral districts from nine to twenty-nine, so as to help his Socialist Party win more parliamentary seats with fewer votes than they had received in previous elections.

That fall, Avramovic was announced as the leader of the opposition coalition, now renamed Zajedno—Together. But a week later, and just one month before election day, he abruptly stepped down, citing age and ill health. Rumor had it that the United States had withheld its support because it felt only Milosevic could ensure that the agreements made in Dayton would not be broken. But Avramovic had also been threatened by one of Milosevic's key advisors, Nikola Sainovic, with corruption charges, falsely accusing him of using his position to obtain lush apartments for himself and his daughter.

Either way, with "Grandpa" out, the opposition foundered at first. With considerable fraudulent assistance behind the scenes, a coalition of Socialists led by Milosevic and a pro-Communist party led by his wife won a comfortable majority in the federal parliament. That being said, there was no clear winner in the municipal elections, where votes were counted on the spot rather than at central locations under the control of the central election board. In a runoff two weeks later, the Zajedno group won the day in thirty-four of the country's largest cities, including Belgrade.

Opposition parties celebrated the unprecedented victories. But with the state propaganda machines spewing bogus election numbers, Milosevic put his operatives to work recounting, stuffing ballot boxes, and even changing votes, then ordered the tallies be reversed. But this was a bridge too far, even for Milosevic—tens of thousands of people took to the streets of Belgrade, demanding that the election results be honored. For eleven frigid weeks, Serbs marched daily through the streets of Belgrade, drumming garbage can lids and armed with whistles, unleashing a deafening racket. From 7:30 to 8:00 p.m. each evening, the whole city seemed to let loose full throttle. Protestors pelted government buildings with eggs. Effigies of Milosevic and his wife were dragged on floats through the streets. Protests spread throughout the country. Much of civil society—schools, universities, and theaters—ground to a halt.

Milosevic seemed stunned by the popular outcry. A senior Western diplomat who called on him at the presidential palace during this tense period reported that "the noise of that day's demonstration could be clearly heard outside his window, which no doubt contributed—as did his substantial whiskey intake—to his mounting anger." When the visitor suggested that the protestors saw the outcome of the elections as an infringement of their basic human rights, the dictator became more agitated. "If you are here to represent your country you are welcome," he threatened, peppering his language with frequent obscenities, "but if you are here to settle the affairs of Serbia, you are not."

Naturally, these protests were largely ignored by the state media. When its reporters did cover the rallies, the TV screens showed only the outer fringes of the crowds and claimed that only a few hundred dissidents were involved plus a few "accidental passersby." In response, many of the protesters began wearing "Accidental Passerby" buttons. Soon, even some of Milosevic's most critical supporters began to rebel. Five members of the Supreme Court openly criticized the use of the legal system to subvert election results. Then Milosevic's minister of information, Aleksandar Tijanic, resigned.

On December 2, I implored President Clinton to exert pressure on Milosevic to honor the results of the local elections, arguing it was a mistake to think that only he could assure the survival of the Dayton agreement. "We cannot let Milosevic believe we need him so badly that we are prepared to overlook his antidemocratic excesses against his own people," I wrote. In response to such efforts, Milosevic sounded his usual litany of nationalist grievance. "Serbia will never be ruled by a foreign hand," he averred, "Serbia will never bow before anyone." But after protests had continued for weeks, an increasingly desperate Milosevic asked me to come see him at his residence. In our first meeting in five years, I said on arrival, "You've lost. You must accept the results." Milosevic replied, "I can't do this. I can't reverse myself now. Can you explain that to the Americans?" "I can't help you," I replied. "You've got to accept the election results."

While Milosevic had long wielded dictatorial power, he had also maintained a pretense of constitutional legitimacy. Now even that flimsy facade was cracking. Pressures were now coming from all sides— from the United States, from neighboring countries, even from Patriarch Pavle, the head of the Serbian Orthodox Church, which mounted the largest religious procession Belgrade had ever seen in support of the protesters. On February 4, Milosevic finally conceded defeat—he would allow the local election results to stand. The loss of Belgrade was particularly galling, but Milosevic privately assured his supporters that the opposition parties would rapidly demonstrate their political incompetence. "They have a plane, but they don't have a pilot," he remarked scornfully.

The opposition took over positions in local councils throughout the country. Zoran Djindjic became the first noncommunist mayor of Belgrade since 1945. I believed that the newly elected opposition leaders deserved strong support from the West. I financed foreign trips by opposition activists and brought Djindjic and Draskovic to Washington to meet with Clinton administration officials. Madeleine Albright, now serving as Clinton's secretary of state, promised Djindjic that she would remove the hold on the desperately needed sum of $8,000,000 belonging to the city of Belgrade currently blocked in U.S. banks. However, when Djindjic returned home, Albright's aides informed him that it could not in fact be done. He had no money to fund basic services for a city of two million people. When Albright visited Belgrade a few weeks later, Djindjic refused to meet with her.

I then wrote letters to both Clinton and Albright, noting that the united opposition front he had helped put together was bound to fail "without the active engagement of the United States and the European Community. . . . And if we fail, the Dayton agreement may well fall apart." Instead, what fell apart was Zajedno. During the protests of the winter, Zajedno leaders had put aside their differences in the shared goal of defeating Milosevic. But the strains of leadership, and the various egos and rivalries among the opposition figures, began to produce fissures. By the end of the spring, just as Milosevic had predicted, Zajedno was crumbling.

To be sure, Milosevic did his part to help. He initiated a secret meeting with Mayor Djindjic, and then leaked information about it to the press. After initial denials, Djindjic was forced to admit meeting the dictator. Other leaders of the opposition side felt betrayed. Then, in the summer of 1997, Milosevic had himself elected president of Yugoslavia by the federal assembly, gaining comfortable majorities in both chambers of parliament—after opposition parties boycotted the event on grounds that the election was unconstitutional.

In early 1997, Montenegro's Djukanovic initiated an open fight with the dictator. "I am convinced that it would be completely politically wrong for Slobodan Milosevic to continue to occupy any post in Yugoslavia's political life," he told an interviewer. "Milosevic today is a man of obsolete political ideas who is not capable of assessing the strategic challenges facing our state." Later that year, in the months before the Montenegrin presidential elections, Milosevic struck back. With control of the federal government in his hands, he tried to provoke civil unrest in the small second part of the nation through an economic boycott. Pauperizing the Montenegrin population would, he assumed, undercut Djukanovic's political popularity.

Djukanovic found himself in an increasingly desperate position. The Clinton government offered moral support, but no cash. I stepped in and personally helped provide funds, which Djukanovic used to pay the salaries of his police force and government bureaucrats. In the end, Djukanovic won—and the following year Montenegro received $55 million in U.S. economic and other aid. But the victory at the polls further frayed the already loose bonds between the Yugoslavian federation of Serbia and Montenegro. Three years later, Yugoslavia would become the short-lived nation of Serbia and Montenegro, and another three after that, both were completely independent of the other. From the elections in 1997 forward, however, few links between the two remained intact.

U.S. support of Djukanovic, however tentative at first, masked growing uncertainties in the Clinton administration on how best to deal with Milosevic. The Dayton agreement had been an important foreign policy achievement for Clinton, who saw Milosevic as crucial to its success. But Holbrooke, Albright, and the State Department's special envoy to the region, Robert S. Gelbard, felt that Milosevic was clearly undermining peace efforts in Bosnia, and not taking the difficult steps needed to ensure that the Bosnian Serbs went along with the deal. Finally, I was being proven right.

To increase pressure on Milosevic, the United States worked to elect a new moderate Serb leadership for the Bosnian Serbs, composed of people not in his direct control. At the same time, Gelbard traveled to Belgrade to deliver a sobering, even melodramatic message—"If you cooperate, you will get a lot more from us," Gelbard told the dictator. "You're at a crossroads. There is one path heading toward the light, and the other will lead you on a spiral toward darkness." From Milosevic's perspective, it seemed no matter what he did, the United States would continue to try to isolate Yugoslavia. While international sanctions were lifted, the United States fought efforts to recognize the country diplomatically and those to allow the country to join international organizations.

And so Milosevic chose his path, and the former Yugoslavia spiraled ever further and faster toward darkness.

12

TROUBLE IN KOSOVO

Back in the United States, I kept up pressure on Washington to do something about Milosevic and to provide more support for his opponents. But by now, politics had lost some of its magic. For years now, I had toiled on behalf of Balkan peace, and it was eating away at what was left of my idealism. Too often now, I had seen the dark side of power— ambitious officials, largely concerned about furthering their careers, eloquently pushing ill-considered schemes over what was really needed at the time. Still, I remained unshaken in my belief in American values. And I had also discovered things about myself. I had a better understanding of who I was, where I'd come from, where I was going, and what it takes to succeed. Asked if I would consider going back by President Clinton, I told him, "I want to help, Mr. President. If you ask me, I will go, but only if I have your support this time."

At the same time, I had a global business to manage: ICN Pharmaceuticals now had fifty-two factories in thirty-one countries. In Russia alone, it had 5 manufacturing plants and 136 pharmacies. Worldwide, it made and marketed some six hundred prescription drugs and sold fifty-five thousand biotechnology research products and medical diagnostics. In 1997, the value of the company's shares on the New York Stock Exchange shot up 152 percent. And I was determined to make it much larger, "the Merck of the future."

At home in Newport Beach, I had additional and pleasurable distractions. My new wife Melena brought people into my circle who preferred art over politics and who induced me to become more in-

volved in cultural activities. I kept the Pasadena mansion that overlooked Caltech's campus and hosted charitable affairs there. And I became one of the Los Angeles Opera's major supporters. Yet, all the
while, the unfinished project in my life gnawed at me—I still harbored
deep concerns about Serbia's future. My commitment was so deep that
it surprised me. I never believed that I could get into this so deeply,
that my emotions would be so involved.

After witnessing the breakdown of Zajedno, and seeing the democratic opposition in Yugoslavia degenerate into narrow careerism and
partisan squabbling, I moved closer to my original views on the subject.
Serbia's political and economic reconstruction, I now thought, depended on its relations with the United States. It became my new
mission to repair Serbia's ties with America while, at the same time,
working with the Serbian opposition to slowly and gradually change the
mind of the nation. The latter, it seemed, was more difficult. The opposition leaders yearned for a rational and urbane society, but they had no
idea how to create it. They needed Western help, I realized, and they
still weren't getting it.

If anything, I thought American diplomacy was making the situation
in the Balkans far worse by ignoring—perhaps because of the lack of
understanding—the tensions in Kosovo, an enclave of more than 1.8
million Albanians and 300,000 Serbs. Even under the best of circum-
stances, the problem seemed nearly unsolvable; but it was particularly
explosive while Milosevic remained in power. In early 1998, I warned
Clinton that Kosovo's unrest would escalate into a serious regional conflict. "I'm deeply troubled," I told the president. "For six years I have
argued that Milosevic is the problem and [that he] cannot perform a
constructive role in any solution. Counting upon him to enforce the
Dayton Accords or to bring about a peaceful resolution of the Kosovo
problem is like counting on the devil to eliminate sin."

Any outbreak of fighting in Kosovo could easily engulf the entire
Balkans in conflict—not only neighboring Albania and Macedonia (both
home to large Albanian populations) but even Greece and Turkey. Of
all the many tinderboxes in the former Yugoslavia, Kosovo was unique.
In Bosnia, intermarriage and the intermingling of societies was the rule,
not the exception. But Kosovo remained a truly divided society, with
opposing languages, schools, and social interactions. From a political
perspective, there was not much room for compromise. The Albanian

Kosovars were clamoring for independence. The Serb authorities were more interested in repression than self-determination.

For Milosevic, Kosovo was an inseparable part of Serbia. The "oppression of Serbs" in the blighted region had sparked his political ascendancy, and he seemed to reserve a special antipathy for the Albanian Kosovars. In his book *Waging Modern War*, General Wesley Clark says Milosevic told him that if trouble began brewing in Kosovo, Serbia knew how to deal with Albanian nationalists—they had done it before. "When was that?" asked Clark. "In Drenica, back in 1946," Milosevic replied. "How did you do it?" Clark said. "We killed all of them. It took several years, but we killed all of them."

The Albanian Kosovars were in a similarly nonconciliatory mood. Albanian schools remained closed. With the local economy in utter disarray, many families lived off remittances sent by relatives working abroad. Frustration and impatience with Serb rule were on the rise. The failure of Dayton to address Kosovo's quest for independence not only strengthened Milosevic. It radicalized many young Albanians, and undermined the peaceful, nonresistance movement of Ibrahim Rugova—the leader I had met with in 1992. Then, our potential agreement had failed because of demonstrations by Seselj and the ultranationalist Serbs and the concern that parliament would vote against any such accord. Now, though the province's intellectual and political elites stood behind Rugova, young people were growing restive—nonviolence wasn't working. Moreover, from the perspective of the Kosovars, the Dayton Accords legitimized secession movements in the Balkans. If the Bosnians could exit Yugoslavia, and the local Serbs could secede from an independent Bosnia, why should the Albanians be any different?

It seemed only a matter of time before Kosovo exploded. Impatient young Kosovars began organizing the Kosovo Liberation Army. Clad in camouflage, brandishing machine guns, and airing the grievances of Kosovo's Albanian minority, the KLA began randomly assassinating Serb officials and police officers. As KLA leaders had to expect, the Serbs responded with fearful, brutal, and often exhibitionistic violence, which the KLA hoped would help further radicalize the Albanian population and create an international outcry. Exactly that happened in February 1998. Serb police killed fifty-four suspected KLA guerrillas and their families in retaliation for the killings of two Serb policemen. When television pictures of the massacre reached Western audiences, they provoked revulsion, raised the specter of another Bosnia-type conflict, and earned the Serbs even more public condemnation.

The KLA was helped enormously by events in neighboring Albania. In the summer of 1997, the nation had descended into chaos and rioting after the collapse of several large-scale pyramid schemes, in which as many as two out of three citizens had invested heavily. Criminal gangs took advantage of the near anarchy, looted the Albanian army's weapons facilities, and smuggled large quantities of weapons into Kosovo. That supply further strengthened the KLA. Milosevic was forced to dispatch more and more troops and police to the province. And soon, civil war began in earnest.

By the early summer of 1998, the KLA controlled nearly 40 percent of Kosovo. Yugoslav troops, ordered into action to "pacify" troublesome rebel strongholds, began taking more brutal measures—burning crops, destroying villages, and massacring civilians. Hundreds of thousands of terrified villagers fled their homes. Some fled across the border to Albania, others into the woods.

Here was yet another missed opportunity in a long, sad history of them. I had been the first Serbian leader to acknowledge Albanian grievances in Kosovo. When I was prime minister I offered what were extraordinary concessions—autonomy, home rule, Albanian-language education, everything except independence. Now, with Milosevic in power, the potential for mass bloodshed was enormous.

Not surprisingly, the United States once again viewed Serbia as the "bad guys" in Kosovo. Certainly, Milosevic's heavy-handed behavior sparked such a view. But this was not just another example of Serbian malfeasance. The Kosovars were seeking independence, and they were using terror tactics to achieve their goals. By failing to take into account the ultimate objectives of Albanians in Kosovo, Macedonia, and beyond, the United States risked taking sides in a conflict far more nuanced than many Western policy makers realized.

Then as always, war was not the answer. Rather, what was needed was a concerted effort to use the levers of political power to unseat Milosevic. Throughout the country, resistance to Milosevic's regime was growing. I wanted to do everything in my power to energize these opposition forces—both to bring democracy to Serbia and to prevent another Balkan war. I revived the Alliance for Change political movement and encouraged its leaders' efforts to start an intensive campaign of grassroots rallies throughout Serbia. In Belgrade itself, peaceful demonstrations continued nightly as student activists formed Otpor (Resistance), which fast became a crucial element of the antigovernment coalition. I even secretly approached top military and security officials of the Milosevic regime in order to gauge their support for the growing opposition.

In the spring of 1998, I opened a government affairs office in Washington and recruited a young Serbian American political operator, Obrad Kesic, to run it. Like me, Kesic was born in Serbia, but he was just two years old when his parents immigrated to East Chicago, Indiana. From his outpost in the U.S. capital, and with a keen appreciation of the difference between the desirable and the possible—not often present among the Milosevic opposition—Kesic began to give my Serbian democracy-building program a clearer organizational direction. He set up, for example, strategy sessions for opposition activists and Otpor members in Montenegro and elsewhere in Eastern Europe.

I also brought back my pollster, Doug Schoen, to take regular readings of the temperature of the Serbian electorate. The numbers were seemingly unchanged from my failed bid in 1992. Milosevic could not win a free and fair election. The opposition parties were small, each polling 2 or 3 percent of the vote. But, united behind a single candidate, they could be a force that would overwhelm Milosevic's coalition of Socialist and Communist parties. Uniting them was another matter, but I believed that if I could somehow get them the full support of the United States, they could demonstrate to Milosevic that another fraudulent election in Serbia would not be accepted.

In July 1998, Scanlan, Bayh, and I met with Bob Gelbard, still the most senior State Department official dealing with Balkan affairs, and convinced him to meet directly with the Alliance for Change leaders. The opposition politicians were picked up by my Boeing 727 and flown to The Hague. Gelbard was initially skeptical about the credibility of the opposition forces, but he came away from the meeting grudgingly convinced of the potential of the Alliance. "We'll look for ways to support these people if they stay together," he told me. The Serbian participants came away ecstatic. The meeting, in effect, conferred legitimacy on the Alliance and boosted the morale of its members.

The Gelbard meeting and subsequent signs of American support were not missed by Milosevic, who responded by tightening his repressive grip on the country even further. A former minister of the interior, a deputy minister of interior, and several top security officials were all assassinated. The autonomy of Belgrade University was curtailed, and faculty members and students friendly to the opposition were harassed. Any remaining provincial radio stations and newspapers were shut down. Of course, Milosevic also tried to weaken the opposition by playing up the fears of Western involvement in the Kosovo conflict and reawakening the never fully latent paranoia about foreign involvement in Serbia's affairs. This spur to nationalism moved many even in the opposition—Vuk Draskovic, who had earlier been held and beaten by the regime, now became a deputy premier in the Milosevic government. Other opposition leaders began to publically agree with Milosevic over the Kosovo issue.

Milosevic also moved directly against me. In 1997, ICN Yugoslavia, by that time accounting for about 60 percent of Yugoslavia's pharmaceutical sales, had made a deal with the state-owned Serbian Health Fund to provide drugs to the Serbian hospitals on credit. By July 1998, the health fund and other Serbian agencies owed ICN nearly $176 million. Although the government owned 25 percent of the company, it said it could not or would not pay the company what it was owed— implying that it would resume payments only if I ceased political activity in Serbia. ICN's shares fell sharply, but the real pain was felt by Serbian hospitals cut off from much-needed pharmaceuticals.

Despite my continued pleading, the mood in Washington began to shift from diplomacy to armed intervention. Along with General Wesley Clark, by then NATO supreme commander, Albright and Holbrooke pushed for the use of force against Serbia. Albright said Milosevic was a "schoolyard bully" who would run the first time his nose was bloodied. Clark insisted that just the threat of an aerial attack would deter Milosevic. In *Waging Modern War*, Clark recalls that he was asked by General Joseph Ralston what would happen if that did not work. Clark replied, "Well, it will work. I know him well as anyone." Ralston persisted: "OK, but let's just say it doesn't. What will we do?" Clark replied, "Well, then we'll bomb. We'll have to follow through." "And what if the bombing doesn't work?" Ralston asked. "I think that's unlikely but in any event, I guess we'd have to do something on the ground, directed at Kosovo."

Not done yet in my pursuit of peace, I established contact with the top generals in Milosevic's security apparatus—Momcilo Perisic, chief of staff; Alexander Dimitrijevic, head of military intelligence; and Jovica Stanisic, chief of internal security. All said they opposed the dictator's confrontational course and certainly did not want to fight NATO. In the early fall, I sent my young aide, Obrad Kesic, to Belgrade to meet with Perisic. The clandestine meeting took place in the general's limousine. "The first thing he wanted to know was if his name was on the list" of Serbian officials secretly indicted by the Hague tribunal, Kesic said later. "We had checked earlier with the State Department and the CIA and I was able to tell him: no, your name is not on the list."

But the Clinton administration had no trust in backroom politics. In October, Holbrooke appeared to have brokered a peace accord when he used the NATO threat to push Milosevic to halt the Kosovo military campaign. Milosevic also allowed 1,600 international inspectors into Kosovo, moved batteries of surface-to-air-missiles, and sanctioned flyovers by NATO spy planes. I still seriously doubted that Milosevic was serious about political change in Kosovo. And I was certain the Albanians had the capacity to sabotage any accord, and would do so now that they had the initiative on the ground and the attention of the United States and its Western allies.

In an October speech at the U.S. Institute of Peace in Washington, I asserted that air attacks "would only worsen the human tragedy in Kosovo by encouraging extremist elements among both Serbs and Albanians, and would exacerbate the problems—not solve them. NATO air strikes against Serbia would further undermine the single force that can bring real change to the Balkans: democracy." At the Institute—and in an open letter to Clinton published as a full-page newspaper ad—I argued that instead of a bombing campaign that would solidify Serbs behind Milosevic, the United States should "by word and deed" help the opposition parties and the government of Montenegro, support a free Serbian media, and insist that Milosevic hold fair elections.

A few weeks later, opposition leaders repeated those arguments before the Helsinki Commission in Washington. When they returned, one of them, Boris Kurajcic, was arrested and tortured. Another, Slavko Curuvija, the editor of an independent weekly, was shot and killed by masked assailants outside his Belgrade home. While I was out of the dictator's reach at that moment, ICN's Yugoslavian subsidiary was not.

In February 1999, it was seized by police and five of its top managers arrested.

Meanwhile in Kosovo, the KLA, as I had warned, looked for ways to keep the situation inflamed. They counted on Serbian overreaction to further isolate Milosevic, increase the demand in the West for NATO action, and thus improve the chances for full independence. In the winter of 1998–1999, KLA forces killed four Serbian policemen in the town of Racak. The violent Serb response handed the KLA a huge propaganda opportunity to present its members as brave freedom fighters confronting a brutal dictatorship. At dawn, the Serbs shelled the village and, although it was a European peacekeeping monitoring location, then entered the town, rounded up some forty-five men, marched them to a nearby gully, and machine-gunned them to death. The head of the Kosovo Verification Mission, which had been set up as part of the Holbrooke agreement to monitor events in the province, called it a "crime against humanity." Holbrooke's arrangement had utterly failed to keep the peace.

The road to war was now open. U.S. officials still seemed to believe that a few days of bombardments would do the job, that Milosevic needed a small NATO attack to create a political cover for his retreat from Kosovo. I told the administration that this was a mirage. I flew to Paris accompanied by Andrei Kozyrev, the former Russian foreign minister who was now a member of the ICN board of directors. With Kozyrev's help, I had gained the Russian government's support for a plan to isolate and remove Milosevic. All the Western allies were now asked to do was to refuse to deal with Milosevic and instead invite Djukanovic and dissident generals in the Yugoslav army to negotiate on behalf of Yugoslavia. But Albright refused to meet with us. Like Holbrooke, she refused to help the opposition.

In February 1999, with the potential for violence ever rising, the United States and its NATO allies brought Serbs and Kosovars together at the former French royal hunting lodge in Rambouillet, outside Paris. The meetings were geared toward ending the violence in Kosovo and moving toward a long-term viable political solution to the crisis. The sides found little to agree upon, with one notable exception: Neither supported the NATO offer.

Both parties were invited to sign a hastily prepared accord under Albright's supervision. The Serbs weren't interested. They opposed a provision that provided for a NATO peacekeeping force in Kosovo. Even more disastrous for Albright, the Kosovars also turned it down. The agreement did not require a referendum on independence. Without the Albanians' support, how could NATO justify a bombing campaign on their behalf?

Finally, after extraordinary American pressure, the Kosovars reluctantly signed on March 18 in Paris. The Serbs still refused. Nevertheless, the United States and NATO agreed to attack Yugoslavia if it failed to abide by an agreement to which it had not agreed. Possibly believing that NATO would never carry out its threat, Milosevic was not impressed even after Holbrooke traveled to Belgrade to warn him that it would. Later Holbrooke would say, "It was Milosevic who deliberately and consciously chose to trigger the bombing of his own country." In fact, I had personally warned Holbrooke that Milosevic would do such a thing.

On the evening of March 24, 1999, as NATO planes were commencing their bombing runs over southeastern Europe, I stood in front of the State Department in Washington, participating in a candlelight protest against U.S. policy. I am a fierce patriot, but I knew that nothing good would come of this war—that the United States was using force as a substitute for the dirty work of building a democratic opposition in Serbia to topple Milosevic. This view troubled even some of my most ardent supporters. Even my friend Bill Press, the longtime liberal writer and commentator, would argue that occasionally there was a time and place for war. But I disagree. For intelligent people, those days should be over. No idea is worth killing for.

War was not only immoral. It was impractical. Instead of weakening the main obstacle to peace, Slobodan Milosevic, it would strengthen the dictator at home. Serbs are patriots. Even those who truly hated Milosevic could not stand with NATO against the Serbian people. Milosevic compared the initial NATO assault on Belgrade to the savage German attacks of 1941—ignoring the fact that then, thousands of Belgrade residents died in a single day, while there were no reports of civilian casualties from the first NATO bombing.

In scores of media interviews, I refused to back down from my criticism of the United States and NATO. "If we did not bomb him," I argued on CNN's *Crossfire*, "he would not stay in power for very long." Milosevic, I said, "is politically finished. He has not won a single election in ten years." In an article for the *Wall Street Journal*, I wrote, "We should isolate Milosevic. We should announce that our quarrel is not with the Serbian nation, it is with Mr. Milosevic. We should say that we recognize and respect the legitimate rights of the Serbian nation, but we no longer recognize Mr. Milosevic as its legitimate leader and will no longer deal with him."

Far from backing down, Milosevic purposely engineered a humanitarian crisis for which NATO was not prepared. He sent his Serbian forces back into Kosovo, massacring Kosovars and forcing them out of their homes. Milosevic had once boasted to Clark that he could empty Kosovo of Albanians in a mere five days—it took a bit longer, but not much. Only a few weeks into the war, three-quarters of the Albanian population were refugees. Hundreds of thousands fled across the borders to Macedonia and Montenegro, a mass movement that Milosevic obviously hoped would also be a problem for his intractable opponent, Djukanovic. In fact, two years later, Albanian refugees, by then a quarter of the population, would prove even more troublesome in Macedonia—starting a civil conflict that verged on civil war and ended when they were granted forms of local autonomy.

My frustration with the United States and NATO kept me in almost constant circulation on the major cable news networks. One television newscaster described me as the "most passionate voice" for the Serbs. "We don't need to destroy the country to get rid of Milosevic," I insisted. "Democratization is the only solution; and you don't teach people democracy by bombing them." I repeatedly rejected allegations that the Serbian people were collectively responsible for "genocide" in Kosovo. The crimes, I argued, were committed by Milosevic's paramilitary thugs—no more, no less.

Meanwhile, Serbia's democratic opposition was effectively paralyzed by the war. They knew that Serbia was bound to lose and that Milosevic's machinations had made the war possible, but found it impossible or at least dangerous to criticize the government. One critic, an independent publisher, was falsely accused of favoring the NATO assault and killed by regime agents. Fearing for their lives, some of the key opposition figures found safe haven in Montenegro. During a television interview, Draskovic, still a deputy minister, accused Milosevic of lying: "The people should know that NATO is not facing a breakdown, Russia will not help Yugoslavia militarily, and that the world public is against us." He could not have been surprised when he was fired the next day.

And the bombing continued. Missiles and bombs demolished almost anything of any military use in Serbia—not only airports, military bases, bridges, heating plants, railway lines and highways, but power grids and factories making everything from cigarettes to shoes. Serbia's economy, already crippled by eight years of sanctions, was completely destroyed. Milosevic's residence was hit by missiles, but the dictator was in hiding. Graffiti appeared around the city saying "Slobo, when we needed you most, you weren't home." On June 3, 1999, with the assistance of Russian negotiators, Milosevic agreed to withdraw all Serbian forces from Kosovo. The province was then occupied by NATO troops and a few Russians and other nationalities, but effectively turned over to the KLA—which set out with ruthless efficiency to rid the province of Serbs who had not already fled. Once again, war had left its terrible mark.

13

FINALLY, GOOD NEWS

Eight days before the end of the Kosovo war, Milosevic and four associates were indicted for war crimes by The Hague–based International Criminal Tribunal for the Former Yugoslavia. The indictment—the first war crimes indictment of a sitting head of state—accused them of responsibility for 340 murders in seven separate massacres, as well as the forced deportation of 740,000 people. Despite this historic proclamation, Milosevic remained in malevolent control of a Serbia where opponents or critics of his policies justly feared for their lives. Some simply disappeared. Ivan Stambolic, who had once been Milosevic's mentor, went jogging in a Belgrade park and never returned. In 2003, when his body was found in a pit outside the city, a court determined that he had been shot by members of the Red Berets, Milosevic's special police unit.

This was clearly not a time for me to be in Belgrade. Instead, I worked from the outside, flying regularly to Montenegro to meet with Serbian opposition leaders. Once again, the only thing they could agree on was that Slobo had to go. But while Milosevic remained unpopular, he was able to tap successfully into a groundswell of patriotic sentiments caused by the NATO bombing campaign, styling himself as the rebuilder of the country he had been primarily responsible for destroying. The opposition tried more street protests. The first, on August 17, 1999, drew a crowd of more than 150,000 people—but, on following days, the numbers dwindled dramatically.

Internationally, Milosevic still had friends in China, Russia, Iraq, and Libya. At home, with his opponents disorganized, cowed, or permanently silenced, Djukanovic of Montenegro appeared to be his only serious challenger. Nonetheless, I began to see an opportunity for change at last. While seemingly uncertain of what to do about it, many U.S. officials had finally been persuaded by Milosevic's actions over Kosovo that peace in the Balkans would never be possible as long as he remained in power. Once again, I became an indefatigable salesman. In July and August, I held a series of meetings with officials at the National Security Council and State Department, as well as with nongovernmental organizations engaged in international efforts to foster democracy, such as the National Democratic Institute for Foreign Affairs and the National Endowment for Democracy.

With anyone who would listen, I shared the results of Doug Schoen's continuing polls, which had been remarkably consistent from 1992 onward. "The fundamental mistake that the United States made was assuming that Milosevic was strong," Schoen said later. "He was never strong, his favorability always hovered around 30 percent." I conceded the opposition was not united, but I also argued that Milosevic could be ousted in a fair election. All that was required to coalesce the trade unions, students, and opposition politicians was a clear signal of U.S. support. "We should do this openly," I argued. "Only seed money is needed."

I had made the same argument hundreds of times over the past decade, but usually my passionate declarations fell on deaf ears. This time, with Milosevic now an international pariah and continued instability in the Balkans threatening to spill over into other nations, U.S. officials at last began to get the message. "Coming out of the bombing, they needed to find some way to work with opposition people in Belgrade," Jack Scanlan said later. Bob Gelbard played a key role in convincing Albright and Berger to support my plan and secure finances.

I then got funding for still another Schoen poll from the National Democratic Institute. In late September 1999, Schoen conducted a benchmark poll for the Serbian opposition, which was then roughly divided between two leaders with two opposing proposals for action. Zoran Djindjic, the former mayor of Belgrade, advocated some form of grassroots movement that would somehow force Milosevic to resign. Vuk Draskovic, who had both been savagely beaten by Milosevic's men and served as the dictator's deputy prime minister during the Kosovo crisis, wanted to challenge him at the polls in an election then scheduled for that fall.

According to Schoen's numbers, the majority of Serbs agreed with Draskovic. They wanted to see Milosevic toppled at the ballot box. However, reported Schoen, Milosevic was vulnerable only if the opposition could unify behind one candidate and one message. But who would be that candidate? While Milosevic's unfavorability ratings were at 70 percent, Draskovic's and Djinjdic's ratings weren't much better. Despite the fact that he had been tortured and imprisoned by Milosevic, Draskovic had lost credibility when he briefly joined Milosevic's government. Djinjdic, who had fallen from favor when he fled Belgrade to the safe environs of Montenegro during the NATO bombings, lost further support when he underlined the opposition's lack of unity by boycotting the meeting at which Schoen presented the results of his poll.

From my perspective, however, Schoen's poll results were good news, and I promptly forwarded them to friends in Washington. Over the next ten months, the United States began funneling $40 million in funds, through the U.S. Agency for International Development, to commercial contractors and nongovernmental organizations to train opposition activists and provide opposition parties with fax machines, computers, and sophisticated voter surveys. Some funds went directly to student groups, labor unions, and independent media outlets. Even heavy metal bands that staged street concerts during voter registration drives got financial support.

On the American side, this undertaking was bipartisan. The National Democratic Institute worked with the Serbian opposition parties and conducted extensive public opinion polls in Serbia. The International Republican Institute organized seminars for activists in Hungary, where it trained some four hundred Serbs in election monitoring techniques. When they returned home, these four hundred trained another fifteen thousand people on how to detect vote-counting and ballot-stuffing scams.

For years, I had wanted to see Milosevic arrested and humiliated—the pain of the 1992 election had never really washed away. But by 2000, I was willing to give him a way to make a graceful exit, if that would put an end to the lawlessness, repression, and economic chaos that was destroying Serbia. "Peace and stability," I wrote in the *Washington Post*, "require the departure of Mr. Milosevic and free and fair elections under close international supervision. To attain this something must be offered in return. The deal that could be offered is a full and final lifting of sanctions and suspension of prosecution of Mr. Milosevic if he and his wife accept permanent foreign exile." The Russians were willing to accept them. But Milosevic was not willing to go. Despite his legions of informers and police, he apparently underestimated the extent to which the opposition was getting trained and organized. In July 2000, he announced that a new round of presidential elections would take place in September.

I now had high hopes that the opposition could topple Milosevic at last. Yet, the polls did little to encourage my optimism. Milosevic's unfavorability rating had dropped from 70 to 59 percent. And the opposition forces weren't doing much better. Only about a third of the electorate supported the Alliance for Democratic Change, the only viable opposition. Part of the general apathy was due to the populace's pessimistic suspicion that no matter what happened, Milosevic would find a way to steal the election as always. Besides, most potential voters had no confidence in the familiar cast of characters who made up the opposition.

If ever there was a time for a fresh face, it was now. Ironically, the idea would come from Djindic. Although he was seen by some as the one man who could beat Milosevic, Schoen's numbers showed otherwise. Schoen recalls that Djindic said to him, "I can't win, can I?" When Schoen told him he couldn't, Djindic asked, "What about Kostunica?" Vojislav Kostunica, the leader of the small Democratic Party of Serbia, had turned down the justice ministry when I formed my first cabinet. In part because he was not well known, he had low unfavorability ratings. And, unlike the other opposition leaders, he was not seen as promoting himself rather than the cause. Schoen and I agreed it would be an inspired choice.

Everything started to click. The opposition was unifying behind Kostunica. And U.S. support, led now by new ambassador to Yugoslavia William Montgomery, was continuing in unprecedented fashion, even to the extent of paying for such things as five thousand cans of spray paint and the special paper for 2.5 million election stickers printed with two words: *Gotov je*—"He's finished." That summed up the entire campaign. Simple and powerful, it focused people's minds on Milosevic, without ever mentioning his name. Soon, it was plastered over Milosevic posters, spray painted on city walls, and written on banners and T-shirts.

The key to an opposition victory, Schoen suggested, would be publicizing the election results as soon as possible on election day. That would undermine any Milosevic effort to steal the election after the fact. Milosevic had already banned the use of exit polls, Schoen's preferred method for getting out results early. Instead, the opposition—with aid from the United States—added more trained poll watchers. Their job would be to immediately forward tabulation results to an independent monitoring group in Belgrade.

Whether due to hubris or miscalculation, Milosevic seemed to have little sense of how radically the political firmament was being transformed. He ran his campaign much as he had in the 1992 race against me. He made few public appearances and, when he did, it was only to speak to crowds of party partisans. There he railed against the opposition, blasting them as tools of the Americans. This time, ironically, the charge was closer to the mark than it was when I had been the candidate—finally, America was helping. But now more and more Serbs were privately blaming Milosevic for the country's ills rather than the United States.

On the morning of September 24, some thirty thousand opposition poll watchers fanned out across the country, tabulating the numbers and forwarding the results back to Belgrade. Based on Schoen's final polling, the opposition released a press release claiming that Kostunica would win the election by more than nine hundred thousand votes. The goal was clear: Convince the electorate that Kostunica had actually won. Any effort by Milosevic to claim otherwise would be viewed with skepticism. By evening, the results funneling into Belgrade were proving the forecast correct. Just after midnight, Kostunica called a press conference to declare that he won a clear majority and was the next president of Yugoslavia. In Belgrade, people danced in the streets until the early hours of the morning.

With outright theft of the election now impossible, Milosevic played for time. His Federal Election Commission declared that Kostunica had won more votes than Milosevic, but not enough to secure victory in the first round. It announced a second runoff for October 8. Based on both Schoen's polls and the poll watchers' tabulations, this was obviously false. Kostunica had won a clear majority. Faced with the choice of another runoff, the opposition said enough. Peaceful protests were organized around the country. There would be no next round.

These were some of the tensest days of my life. I got on the phone to congressional leaders, to the White House, to anyone who had direct links to the president, appealing for full American support. "You are dealing with a guy who is a master at stealing elections," I told President Clinton. "We mustn't let him get away with it this time." Relentless outside pressure would both limit the dictator's capacity for mischief and further embolden the democratic forces in Serbia. This time, I argued, America had to make it clear that the Western world was not going to accept a fraudulent outcome.

On the morning of October 5, only days before the scheduled bogus runoff, thousands of protestors from around the country converged in Belgrade. Slobodan Milosevic ordered police and security forces to stymie the crowd. Nonetheless, thousands of people gathered outside the parliament building, chanting slogans and calling on the dictator to step down. At one point, a protestor arrived with a bulldozer and the crowd followed it, seizing the building and setting it afire. Next went the television station. Even Milosevic loyalists could sense which way the political wind was blowing. The generals kept their troops in the barracks. The police simply withdrew from the burning parliament. That night Kostunica addressed a cheering crowd with a simple, but long overdue greeting, "Good evening, liberated Serbia." The following day, Milosevic conceded defeat. On Saturday, October 6, 2000, Vojislav Kostunica was sworn in as the newly and fairly elected president of Yugoslavia.

I got the news in a Berlin hotel, where Melena was scheduled to perform. I must have spent hours literally jumping and down, calling friends, and extolling Milosevic's loss. It had taken much longer than I had ever imagined, and taken more out of me than I had even thought possible. But, on that day, the work of eight grueling years came to fruition: Democracy had come to the former Yugoslavia at last. With that fateful step taken, the ghosts of the past that had tormented Serbia for centuries could finally begin to be exorcised, and the economic opportunity, tolerance of diversity, and other American ideals that I had wanted to bring to my native land for so long could start to take root.

Forty-five years after I had left my home in Serbia to follow the future, I had finally helped to bring that future back.

For Jack Scanlan, the day was a bit more bittersweet. He was in Minnesota attending the funeral of his older sister. When he returned to his motel, he was stunned by the pictures he saw on CNN. "I almost couldn't believe I was seeing what I was seeing," he said to me later. For all his joy, there was a tinge of sadness. "I felt we could have done the same thing in 1992, had Bush and Baker supported us."

How many Serbs, Croats, Bosnians, Kosovars, and Montenegrins had died or lost their homes, because the United States had withheld its support from me for so long?

* * *

Jack is gone now. My dear friend passed in 2007, at the age of seventy-nine, after complications from a fall. But the question he raised still haunts me today. Serbia and all of the former Balkan states are in a better place now. They are freed from the shadows of Communism and Milosevic, and unshackled from so many of the burdens of the past. Now these new nations can look to the horizon and build their own futures, as neighbors in peace, goodwill, and prosperity. But the price should never have been so high.

Jack and I took so many risks to achieve peace in the Balkans. As prime minister, I came to Belgrade ready to tear up the map and give away every concession if it could stop the killing and give the people of the Balkans the freedom to pursue their own way forward. But we were stymied at every turn—not just by Milosevic, not just by warring ethnic leaders, but by U.S. and European officials who preferred caution and the Grand Diplomatic Game to actually working toward the great goal of peace.

To this day, I wish that Baker and Eagleburger, Owen and Vance, Albright and Holbrooke, and Bush and Clinton had listened to my warnings about Milosevic, or appreciated what Jack and I were trying to do in my former home of Yugoslavia. So much of that terrible decade of the 1990s—all the death and destruction that engulfed the Balkans and made a horror of Srebrenica—could have been averted if the diplomats and world leaders had been willing to take greater risks for peace. In the end, nothing is more important.

ACKNOWLEDGMENTS

All books are a collaborative effort, and this one more than most. There are many who have been indispensable to this project over the years, without whom this book would never have seen the light of day. Here is a brief—too brief—chance to thank them.

First, I want to thank all the dear friends and colleagues who took the time to speak with me about our journeys together, and who offered their honest thoughts and memories about this contentious period in our lives, among them Birch Bayh, David Calef, David Owen, Bill Press, Roberts Smith, and Sally Panic. This is a stronger book for their wisdom and insights.

Most of all, I want to thank my dear, departed friend and comrade for peace, the late Jack Scanlan. His thoughts, research, counsel, and intimate understanding of both Serbian history and the many diplomatic issues we faced while in office and in exile form much of the backbone of this book. In composing this memoir as in so many other things, I could not have done this without him. Thank you for everything, Jack.

I am also deeply indebted to the work and contributions of Kevin C. Murphy, as well as several other writers who helped me to gather my thoughts in book form, among them Yugoslavia expert and former *Washington Post* Moscow bureau chief Dusko Doder and Michael Cohen, a former State Department speechwriter and long-term writer and observer on foreign affairs. Phillip Siekman also provided invaluable aid, research, and editing.

My good friend Bill Press was gracious enough not to only be interviewed, but to write the foreword for this book. His kindness is much appreciated as well.

Over more than thirty years, I have been blessed with the invaluable assistance of two very talented and dedicated executive assistants. Marcia O'Hagan joined our team at ICN in 1978 and quickly became leader of the team. A first-class manager, she helped me navigate my way through the world of business and California politics—and then left her home and family to join me in Yugoslavia through all the excitement, risks, and challenges of my term as prime minister—maintaining her cool even when we came under fire from the Serbian police. I couldn't have done it all without her. She remains an invaluable friend and associate.

Alexandra Novak came to work for me in 1992. Since then, she has been a critical advisor and collaborator on all matters pertaining to politics and business. Her counsel, insights, and tenacity over the years have been invaluable, and she has been instrumental in the creation of this book.

Finally, I want to dedicate this book to my children—Dawn, Milan Jr., Vickie, and Milan Spencer—and to the memory of all the many victims of the Balkan wars and the cruelty and oppression of Slobodan Milosevic's regime. In the words of American poet W. H. Auden, "There is no such thing as the State and no one exists alone. . . . We must love one another or die. . . . May I, composed like them of Eros and of dust, beleaguered by the same negation and despair, show an affirming flame."

Milan Panic, 2014

WHAT HAPPENED TO?

Milan Panic: I returned to Belgrade three days after Milosevic conceded defeat to congratulate Kostunica and his allies, as well as to launch what would be a successful effort to return the Galenika pharmaceutical business to ICN control. But I was still facing criticism from the U.S. Securities and Exchange Commission and discontented shareholders. In 2001, dissidents won three seats on ICN's twelve-member board of directors. The following year, when they increased their positions on the board to six, I resigned as chairman and CEO of the company I had founded and managed for half a century, at the age of seventy-two.

A year later, unable to rest on the sidelines, I struck an agreement with ICN—shortly to be renamed Valeant Pharmaceuticals International. In exchange for most of my shares of ICN stock, I obtained ownership of the company's biomedicals subsidiary, which manufactures and markets research and diagnostic products—the very same business, now vastly expanded by internal growth and acquisitions, which I had started in my garage as a young man. Renamed MP Biochemicals LLC, the company has manufacturing and sales operations in the United States, Europe, and Asia.

Slobodan Milosevic was arrested by Yugoslav authorities on charges of corruption, abuse of power, and embezzlement six months after he conceded defeat in the September 2000 election. When the initial investigation stalled, he was sent to The Hague to stand trial at the International Criminal Tribunal for genocide and crimes against humanity. With Milosevic representing himself, the trial was still under way in

March 2006, when he died of a heart attack. His body was returned to Belgrade for a farewell ceremony and then to his hometown, Pozarevac, for burial.

The services were attended by thousands of people, but Milosevic's wife, Mirijana Markovic, was not among them. She and their son, Marko, moved to Russia shortly after Milosevic was arrested, where they remain as refugees. Serbian authorities have called for their arrest on charges of fraud and murder.

John D. Scanlan served as an officer or consultant to ICN for several years before retiring. He died in 2007 at the age of seventy-nine, after being injured in a fall.

Lawrence Eagleburger died in 2011 of pneumonia at the age of eighty. Both he and *James Baker* served on the Iraq Study Group in 2006, and continued to make frequent comments on foreign policy.

Dobrica Cosic continued to write fiction, comment on political events, and blame the chaos of the 1990s on any and all with the exception of Serbs. "During the brutal war in Bosnia," he wrote in 2011, "only the Bosnian Serb military command behaved with honor and chivalry." He passed away in May 2014.

Birch Bayh, *Doug Schoen*, and *Bill Press* all continue to successfully ply their trades in Washington, D.C., as lawyer, pollster, and television talk-show host respectively.

Vojislav Kostunica served as president of Yugoslavia until 2003, then as prime minister of Serbia from 2004 to 2008 when he dissolved the parliament and called for elections in an effort to gain support for his opposition to an independent Kosovo. He and his followers lost the elections to a pro-European coalition.

Zoran Djindjic became prime minister of Yugoslavia in 2001, played a major role in dispatching Milosevic to The Hague, and was assassinated in March 2003 by a former Red Beret.

Vuk Draskovic struggled politically until his small Serbian Renewal Movement became part of a successful coalition in the 2003 parliamentary election. Since then he has served as foreign minister for both Serbia and Montenegro and, later, Serbia.

Milo Djukanovic served as president of Montenegro from 1998 to 2002 and as prime minister of Montenegro from 2003 to 2006, 2008 to 2010, and 2012 to the present. Over that time, he helped to shepherd his country to full independence, which took place in 2006.

Dusan Mitevic died in 2003. "The things that happened at state TV," he said before his death, "warmongering, things we can admit to now: false information, biased reporting. That went directly from Milosevic to the head of TV."

Dragoslav Avramovic returned to his home in Rockville, Maryland, and died, at eighty-one, in 2001. He was returned to Serbia for burial.

Ibrahim Rugova became president of Kosovo in 2002 and continued to campaign for Kosovo's complete independence from Serbia and for closer relations with the United States and the European Union. In 2005, he was unhurt when a bomb went off as his car passed by, but he died of lung cancer in January 2006.

Radovan Karadzic, Ratko Mladic, and *Vojislav Seselj* have been indicted for war crimes and crimes against humanity and are being held in The Hague by the International Criminal Tribunal for the Former Yugoslavia. Seslj surrendered voluntarily in February 2003, Karadzic was captured in July 2008, Mladic in May 2011. Their trials are still proceeding as of the date of publication.

Franjo Tudjman was still president of Croatia when he died of cancer in December 1999. Had he lived, he very likely would have been indicted for war crimes.

APPENDIX

THE 12 PRINCIPLES OF PEACE, AUGUST 1992

In an August 12 letter to Chinese Ambassador Li Daoyu, Prime Minister Panic put forth his "twelve principles of peace" in the former Yugoslavia—including opposition to the use of force, an acceptance of Tito's borders, rejection of ethnic cleansing, full cooperation with human rights investigators, and UN monitors at all border crossings and military airfields. These principles, crafted by Panic himself with assistance from former ambassador to Yugoslavia John Scanlan, would form the basis of the final agreement reached at the London Peace Conference later that month.

27 AUGUST 1992

PRINCIPLES FOR PEACE
PROPOSED BY PRIME MINISTER MILAN PANIC,
FEDERAL REPUBLIC OF YUGOSLAVIA

1. The Government of Yugoslavia firmly and categorically opposes the use of force to change borders between countries.

2. The Government of Yugoslavia accepts Tito's borders between the republics of his Socialist Yugoslavia as the official international borders between the Federal Republic of Yugoslavia and its neighbouring countries, and states that it has no territorial claims on any of its neighbours.

3. Yugoslavia formally recognized Slovenia on 12 August 1992.

4. Yugoslavia recognizes the state of Bosnia and Herzegovina within its existing internationally recognized borders and has no territorial claims on Bosnia and Herzegovina.

5. Yugoslavia has no territorial claims on Croatia and would like to enter into direct negotiations with Croatia for mutual recognition.

6. Yugoslavia accepts its border with Macedonia as final and has no claims of any kind on Macedonia.

7. Yugoslavia categorically rejects the barbaric practice of ethnic cleansing in any form and all of its tragic consequences, and will bring to justice any Yugoslav citizen against whom it obtains evidence of having engaged in any act of ethnic cleansing. Yugoslavia will co-operate fully and freely with any international investigation into ethnic cleansing.

8. Yugoslavia will welcome and co-operate fully and freely with any international investigation into human rights violations in the republics of the former Socialist Federal Republic of Yugoslavia.

9. The Government of Yugoslavia is conducting its own investigation into human rights violations of its citizens, particularly in Kosovo, Vojvodina and Sandzak. All laws, regulations and administrative practices will be carefully examined and appropriate changes will be made where necessary to ensure that there is no legal or administrative basis for the violation or limitation of the human rights of any citizen of Yugoslavia. The situation in Kosovo will be addressed with a special sense of urgency with the goal of quickly eliminating all human rights abuses.

10. Yugoslavia will co-operate in any way it can to ensure the peaceful delivery of humanitarian aid relief supplies to the people of Bosnia and Herzegovina. It offers the currently greatly under-utilized facilities of Belgrade International Airport for this purpose free of charge, from where relief supplies can be delivered quickly and safely by road to the outskirts of Sarajevo and other cities en route between Belgrade and Sarajevo. Yugoslavia would also participate in such a relief effort with food and medicines from its own reserves.

11. Yugoslavia believes that the refugees from the civil war in Croatia and Bosnia and Herzegovina should be assisted in returning to and rebuilding their homes and will co-operate in this effort in any way it can. There are at present over 400,000 refugees in Yugoslavia who are being assisted and cared for by relatives, friends, good Samaritans, the International Red Cross and agencies of the Yugoslav Government.

12.   As Prime Minister and Minister of Defence of Yugoslavia, I have taken
       all the steps available to me to try to ensure that no support for the
       combatants in the civil war in Bosnia and Herzegovina is coming from
       Yugoslavia. But past history teaches us that there is no paucity of
       people willing to profit from this kind of a situation. Therefore, as I
       said in my letter of 6 August 1992 to the President of the United
       Nations Security Council, I would appreciate the assistance of the
       United Nations in monitoring all of the border crossings between
       Yugoslavia and Bosnia and Herzegovina. I would like to repeat my
       request of 6 August for the United Nations to establish observer posts
       at all of our border crossing points with Bosnia and Herzegovina and my
       request of July 21 1992 to the President of the Security Council for the
       establishment of United Nations observers at all Yugoslav Army air
       fields.

(Excerpt from letter of Prime Minister Milan Panic to the Honourable Li Daoyu,
President of the United Nations Security Council, dated 17 August 1992)

MEMORANDUM OF CONVERSATION, NOVEMBER 1994

Well after his ouster by Slobodan Milosevic, Prime Minister Panic met with President Bill Clinton and his advisors in Anaheim, California. It was at this fateful meeting that Panic planted the seed of inviting all the leaders of the former Yugoslavia to America for an intensive diplomatic dialogue, far away from the political and ethnic pressures in the Balkans. This seed later grew into the historic Dayton peace summit held at Wright-Patterson Air Force Base, near Dayton, Ohio, in November 1995.

MEMORANDUM OF CONVERSATION

BETWEEN PRESIDENT CLINTON AND MILAN PANIC

Participants: President William J. Clinton
               Milan Panic, President, ICN Pharmaceuticals, Inc.
               Sen. Birch Bayh, ICN Board Member
               Amb. John D. Scanlan, ICN VP, Eastern Europe
               Harold Ickes, Jr., Deputy White House Chief of Staff
               Tony Coelho, Counselor to the President

Date: November 5, 1994

Location: Anaheim Convention Center, Anaheim, California

Subject: Yugoslavia

     President Clinton warmly welcomed Mr. Panic and said he was
always interested in hearing his views.

     After some introductory pleasantries, Senator Bayh said he had
been designated to provide a brief foundation for the discussion of
the situation in Yugoslavia. He pointed out that he and Amb.
Scanlan had served respectively as political adviser and foreign
affairs adviser to Mr. Panic during his incumbency as Yugoslav
Prime Minister, and during his election campaign against Slobodan
Milosevic. Birch emphasized that in these capacities they had
observed first-hand the various peace initiatives of Mr. Panic, as
well as his determination and effectiveness as a leader. Birch
pointed out that Ambassador Scanlan was the most important member
of Mr. Panic's team and was indispensable to his efforts.

     Birch said he regretted to see the President inherit such a
difficult situation in Bosnia. This was a direct result of the
previous administration, President Bush and Secretary Baker,
recognizing the various republics at the time of the independence
movements, without previously extracting a political agreement.
President Clinton immediately showed interest and a great awareness
of this, saying that, "In effect, we gave them something for
nothing."

     Birch continued by saying that for a lengthy period of time,
the Administration refused to take Mr. Panic and his government
seriously, and missed an excellent opportunity to shape the course
of events toward peace. When they finally recognized that Mr.
Panic was a much more acceptable, viable alternative to Milosevic,
their comments made the situation more difficult for Mr. Panic,

rather than help him in his efforts against Milosevic.

As an example of the role Mr. Panic played in pursuing the peace process, Birch recalled a dinner with Secretary Cy Vance in Belgrade. Vance indicated the major problems he was having with Milosevic. The following day, Panic, Scanlan and he had a three or four hour session with Milosevic during which Mr. Panic, not yet Prime Minister-designate, argued vociferously with Milosevic that he had to take the steps necessary to meet the points which had been raised the night before by Secretary Vance. Milosevic had to cooperate with the United Nations and accept peace-keeping forces in those Serb pockets of Croatia. The following day, during Vance's negotiating session with Milosevic, Milosevic finally agreed to accept Vance's points and permitted the U.N. peace-keeping forces to assume their positions. The Blue Helmets soon arrived and undertook their responsibilities.

Birch concluded the introductory remarks by emphasizing that, although Mr. Panic is no longer personally involved in Yugoslavian politics, he maintains his contacts there, is extremely well-informed of developments, and is able to exercise considerable influence. The particular reason for this opportunity to discuss the situation was to give Mr. Panic the opportunity to relay to the President the specific information he had picked up the week before while he was in Belgrade.

Mr. Panic said he had been in Belgrade the previous week and believed the moment was ripe for peace. He said everyone there now wants peace but no one knows how to put it together. This can only bee done by a world leader and the President would be the best one to do it.

Together with Mr. Cosic, he had spoken to Karadzic, who wants to find a way but needs something to save face. Karadzic accepts the contact group's proposed division of land, 51%-49%. This willingness had not been publicized previously and amounted to a considerable concession since the Bosnian Serbs presently held approximately 70% of the land area. Mr. Panic pointed out that prior to the outbreak of hostilities, the Bosnian Serbs had been located in about 60% of the territory. They were farmers and peasants and, thus, were widely dispersed over a large percentage of the territory. Mr. Panic pointed out that Mr. Karadzic and the Bosnian Serbs need to have some token of compromise in order to ensure that the contact group agreement is supported by the Bosnian Serb population. The Bosnian Serbs need to get the same provisions as the Croatians, to have the opportunity to federate with Serbia. In addition, they also need to have some status in Sarajevo. There needs to be agreement on some kind of division of the city between the Serbs and the Muslims, not necessarily with specific borders, possibly an open city, something that shows a sharing of Sarajevo. Mr. Panic also said that he was convinced that President Milosevic could be convinced to have open and free elections in Serbia run by the United Nations.

Panic emphasized that the President could address this situation as he has with other crises. Panic suggested that the President consider inviting all of the (former) Yugoslav leaders to meet in the U.S., perhaps at Camp David. Panic suggested that he could get the Serbs to come, and if they agree, the Muslims and the Croats would have to agree. He suggested that Grigorov and Kucan also be invited.

The President said that Milosevic would come because he has to in order to survive, but he then asked whether the Bosnian Serbs would come.

Mr. Panic answered that he was certain Karadzic would come. However, he hoped the President would be able to convince the Muslims to come. Mr. Panic then added that the Serbian people need to hear from the President that we, in the U.S., do not hold them collectively responsible for the policies of their leaders. We had done that with the Haitians. They weren't bad people, it was the leaders' policies that were bad. The Serbian people need to hear that we remember and respect our long history of good relations with them, allies in two world wars, and that we want to work with them if their leaders change their policies and make peace.

The President smiled and said that he fully understood the necessity of this. He pointed out that the most significant thing in his entire Middle Eastern trip was the one sentence in his address to the Jordanian parliament when he said, "We in the U.S. respect Islam." The President said it was like a lightening bolt. The Jordanians had not expected this and applauded enthusiastically.

At this point, Birch returned to the free election issue and asked Panic if he really thought Milosevic could be persuaded to agree to new elections under United Nations supervision with free media. Whereupon, Panic said he was sure Mr. Milosevic would agree as a part of a peace settlement. This might help Milosevic survive for awhile, which was unfortunate. He did not like what Milosevic had done. He had opposed him and fought him. But for now there is no one else, so we have to work with him.

Here President Clinton interjected that he was sure Milosevic would agree to something like this, but how could we deliver the Bosnian Serbs. Mr. Panic said that he could deliver them. Whereupon, Birch recalled a specific incident that illustrated the kind of influence Mr. Panic has been able to have on Karadzic and his klan. At the time of the heaviest shelling of Sarajevo, Mr. and Mrs. Panic were at the Bayh's house in Washington over the 4th of July holiday. In the middle of the night, Mr. Panic awakened and asked that someone get Karadzic on the telephone. Mr. Panic had not met Mr. Karadzic prior to that time. They did find Mr.

3

Karadzic and he and Mr. Panic had a lengthy conversation in which Mr. Panic ordered him to stop the shelling of the airport. He pointed out this was foolish and was really very detrimental to the Serb cause. Karadzic said he would see what could be done. The following afternoon, Karadzic called Panic at the Bayh home and Birch listened in on an extension. Karadzic said that the shelling would stop at 4:00 p.m. the next afternoon. It did and the airport was opened.

Mr. Panic ended his presentation by pointing out that the real problem in the former Yugoslavia is economic. Several mini-economies have been created which cannot survive without cooperating with each other. They won't do this voluntarily and we must help them do it. They will all expect our economic assistance, and it will be much cheaper and more efficient to help them form a free trade association to begin the process of regional economic cooperation, which should include neighboring states as well. The President said that he thought this was an idea that certainly was worth pursuing.

The President said that it was always good to hear from Mr. Panic. He would think about what Panic had said and make some phone calls and see what could be done. All in the Panic party thanked the President for taking time to visit with us.

4

ALONG THE LINES PROPOSED IN YOUR RECENT LETTER, OCTOBER 1995

In this October 3, 1995, letter, President Clinton thanks Panic for his continued advice and advocacy on behalf of the Balkans, and tells the former prime minister he is "considering the idea of a Balkan peace conference along the lines proposed in your recent letter"—reflecting Panic's critical role in the creation of the Dayton peace conference.

THE WHITE HOUSE

WASHINGTON

October 3, 1995

Dear Mr. Panic:

It was a pleasure to see you again in California
and to hear your views on the Balkan conflict.
My foreign policy team and I have been
considering the idea of a Balkan peace
conference along the lines proposed in your
recent letter.

Since we met, our negotiators, working in
concert with the Russians and our other European
partners, have made another important step
forward in the search for a settlement in
Bosnia. On September 26 in New York, we and the
Contact Group hosted a second meeting of the
foreign ministers of Bosnia, Croatia and the
Federal Republic of Yugoslavia. At that
meeting, the three foreign ministers endorsed
additional "Agreed Basic Principles" for a
political settlement in Bosnia, building on the
results of their earlier meeting in Geneva on
September 8. Taken together, these principles
affirm that Bosnia will remain a single state,
with continuing international recognition, made
up of two entities, the Federation and the Serb
Republic. The parties have now agreed on the
governing structures of the Bosnian state and
committed to holding free democratic elections
under international supervision. I have
instructed Ambassador Holbrooke and his team to
return to the region to follow up on the New
York agreement and tackle the remaining
constitutional and territorial issues.

As we come closer to a settlement, we envisage a
high-level conference of the sort you propose
involving Russia, the rest of the Contact Group

and the leaders of Bosnia, Croatia and the FRY.
Such a conference may, indeed, be necessary to
convince the parties to make the hard decisions
needed to resolve the most contentious issues
and to clear the way to a final settlement.

Thank you again for sharing your thoughts on how
to achieve our common goal of a peaceful and
lasting solution to the Balkan conflict.

                    Sincerely,

                    Bill

The Honorable Milan Panic   *Phan call or*
ICN Pharmaceuticals   *wish if you*
3300 Hyland Avenue   *have further comments*
Costa Mesa, California   92626

THE REASON FOR INSTABILITY, NOT THE INSURER OF STABILITY, DECEMBER 1996

In this December 1996 letter to President Clinton, Panic underscores two of his frustrations with American diplomatic maneuvers in the former Yugoslavia: the continuing central presence of Slobodan Milosevic in American peace initiatives and the failure of the West to provide political support to the growing democratic opposition in Serbia.

Republique Federale de Yougoslavie
le Premier Ministre (1992-93)
Milan Panic

December 2, 1996

<u>SENT VIA FAX AND FEDERAL EXPRESS</u>

Dear Mr. President,

I have just returned from 10 days in Belgrade and I would like to share with you my views on the political crisis there. I believe that it is deadly serious and likely to be prolonged, with a potential for unpredictable incidents which could spark a tragic conflict between the Milosevic regime and the surging political opposition.

I am sure you are pursuing various channels of quiet diplomacy to exert pressure on Milosevic to avoid the use of force and to find a way to honor the wishes of the electorate.

I am disturbed, however, by press accounts and analyses saying the west believes that it needs Milosevic to ensure stability and implementation of the Dayton peace accords. Milosevic's policies have been the principle source of instability and conflict in the Balkans for the past six years. He is a masterful tactician and a power-hungry survivor. But he continues to be the reason for instability, not the insurer of stability.

His tactical opportunism and absolute control of Yugoslavia's security and military forces, as well as the purse strings for the Bosnian Serbs made him an essential and useful partner to achieve the Dayton peace accords. You will recall that I acknowledged the need to deal with him and even advocated a Camp David-type scenario when I met with you in Anaheim in early November 1994. However, I believe it is a mistake to think that only he can bring the Bosnian Serbs into line at this point. Zoran Djindjic has much greater influence with the Bosnian Serbs and he has repeatedly assured me -- most recently on November 30 – that he will use that influence to ensure full compliance with the Dayton accords.

Our media tend to brand Djindjic and Vuk Draskovic Serbian nationalists. It is true that both have been outspoken nationalists in the past. Vuk, during the 1990 elections, but not since. Djindjic, more recently in order to undermine Milosevic's and Seselj's public support. But in every country, including the United States, there is a difference between positive nationalism and destructive nationalism. Neither Draskovic nor Djindjic has ever supported the evil excesses of militant Serbian nationalism and destructive nationalism. Milosevic was its Godfather.

Letter to President Clinton
December 2, 1996
Page two

Vuk Draskovic and Zoran Djindjic have matured politically very much during the past four years. Four years ago I tried to unite all of the political opposition leaders in Yugoslavia. They all did support me in my challenge of Milosevic for the Serbian presidency. But they refused to agree to a common slate of candidates for the parliament. Now they are united, as the Zajedno (together) name of their movement indicates. And their popular support is growing rapidly. There are many who would work with them to form an effective government based on free market democratic values and policies. Among them are strong leaders with international credentials, such as Dr. Ljubisa Rakic and Professor Vlastislav Matejic, who work with me at our ICN plant in Belgrade.

Djindjic and Draskovic have appealed to me for support, most recently on November 30. They understand that at this point it would probably be counter-productive for me to get publicly involved. They have assured me that they are not revolutionaries. They want to avoid a clash. But they and their supporters insist that they be permitted to take the offices in government to which they were elected. They are disappointed at the lack of clear western support for this democratic goal.

I recognize that the situation on the ground in Bosnia must be given careful consideration as we consider our policy options with regard to the tense situation in Yugoslavia. However, I believe that we cannot let Milosevic believe that we need him so badly that we are prepared to overlook his anti-democratic excesses against his own people.

I would like to come to Washington this week to discuss this problem in greater detail with your senior foreign policy advisers. I am, as always, prepared to do anything I can to help you in Yugoslavia.

Sincerely,

Milan Panic

William Clinton
President of the United States
The White House
1600 Pennsylvania Avenue
Washington, DC 20500

MP:jac

THE ALLIANCE FOR CHANGE, DECEMBER 1998

In a 1998 open letter to President Clinton, published in the *Washington Times*, Panic once again tries to drum up Western support for Serbia's democratic opposition, now reconstituted as "the Alliance for Change, the broadest-based Democratic coalition in Serbia's recent political history."

The Washington Times

★ THURSDAY, DECEMBER 10, 1998 / PAGE A25

True Peace in the Balkans Will Require Democracy In Serbia

Dear President Clinton:

We want you to know there are Serbs who appreciate the tremendous investment of money, resources and prestige by the United States and the entire international community in trying to build peace and stability in the Balkans. However, all of this effort will be for naught without democracy — the one force that will free Serbia from the fear, brutality and corruption that has plagued it over the last decade.

The Alliance for Change, the broadest-based democratic coalition in Serbia's recent political history, is pushing for comprehensive political and economic reforms in Serbia. We know that there is only one way for democracy to have a chance — Milosevic must go.

We will be moving ahead. Your assistance will help. As our members rally support for elections and democratic change in Serbia during the coming year, we ask that the United States:

- **Support** democratic alternatives to the current regime;
- **Support** our call for general elections through political and diplomatic pressure;
- **Push** the regime of Yugoslav President Slobodan Milosevic to end its monopoly on information and its repression of the independent media;
- **Instruct** senior officials who go to Serbia to meet with representatives of the democratic opposition and to demonstrate clear and unequivocal support for change in Serbia;
- **Develop** a comprehensive international aid program for independent media, free municipalities, university professors and students, trade unions and opposition parties and grassroots movements;
- **Increase** economic assistance to Montenegro, which has come to symbolize the struggle for democracy in the eyes of many citizens of the Federal Republic of Yugoslavia.

We are determined that Serbia will assume its rightful place in the community of free and democratic nations. We ask you to show firm support for our efforts and those of the overwhelming majority of Serbia's citizens who desire a life free of conflict and fear.

On behalf of the Alliance for Change,

Milan Panic
Former Prime Minister of Yugoslavia,
for the Alliance for Change

The Alliance for Change is a loose, liberal democratic coalition of parties and individuals whose common interest is the democratization of Serbia. The coalition is composed of Milan Panic, Dragoslav Avramovic, The Democratic Party, The Civic Alliance of Serbia, The Democratic Alternative, Social Democracy, The Democratic Christian Party and "Srbija - Zajedno."

INDEX

ABOUT THE AUTHORS

Milan Panic is the founder, chairman, and CEO of MP Biomedicals LLC, headquartered in Costa Mesa, California, and the former founder, chairman, and CEO of ICN Pharmaceuticals. A former WWII partisan and champion cyclist in Yugoslavia, Panic moved to California in 1956 with $20 in his pocket and became a self-made millionaire and renowned and successful businessman the world over. He served as the prime minister of Yugoslavia from 1992 to 1993.

Kevin C. Murphy has worked behind the scenes in Democratic politics for the past seventeen years, as a speechwriter, ghostwriter, researcher, editor, and advisor. Over that time, he has written for pundits, strategists, historians, Cabinet officials, and members of Congress. He holds a PhD in history from Columbia University and lives in Washington, D.C.